Love, Race, & *Liberation:*
'Til The White Day is Done

EDITED BY
JLOVE CALDERON AND MARCELLA RUNELL HALL

Love-N-*Liberation* Press
New York

For related titles and support materials, visit our online catalog at www.jlovecalderon.com or www.marcellarhall.com.

To obtain permission(s) to use material from this work, please submit a written request to New York University's Center for Multicultural Education and Programs, 60 Washington Square South, New York, NY 10012 or fax your request to 212-995-3134.

Between the time website information is gathered and then published, it is not unusual for some sites to have closed. Also, the transcription of URLs can result in typographical errors. The publisher would appreciate notification where these errors occur so that they may be corrected in subsequent editions.

ENDORSEMENTS

"*Love, Race, and Liberation* is an essential resource for all of us who care about justice. I'm thrilled to see this visionary but very hands-on and accessible curriculum because it is creative, inspiring, and comes from a loving place dedicated to our collective liberation. Don't just read this book, use it!"
--Paul Kivel, social justice educator, activist, and author of *Uprooting Racism: How White People Can Work for Racial Justice* (www.paulkivel.com)

"*Love, Race, and Liberation* helps to pull all of us, regardless of race, from the societal stupor of a systemic racism that is taken for granted and therefore threatens to become frozen in time as the status quo. The curriculum guides and the letters of conscience allow teacher and student, Black or white, to take a learning and liberating journey, past the untruths and fear of the unknown that have plagued the American discourse on race for centuries. It makes a conversation about race possible, a conversation between people about people. The insights presented in this work, founded in skilled pedagogy, will help teachers and parents facilitate a transformational learning experience that is really more about the future than the past."
--Dr. Perry Greene, Associate Provost for Faculty Affairs at Adelphi University

"*Love, Race, and Liberation* is aptly titled, for it compassionately and non-judgmentally investigates issues of "race" and "race" relations by providing a curricular framework to further awareness, understanding, and liberatory transformation. This is a critical resource for anyone interested in advancing the cause of human relations and social justice."
--Dr. Warren J. Blumenfeld, Department of Curriculum and Instruction, Iowa State University, and Co-editor of *Readings for Diversity and Social Justice*, Second Edition (Routledge, 2010)

"Race in America is complicated—and the role that Caucasian Americans play in it is like the craziest game of Twister you've ever seen. But with *Love, Race, and Liberation: 'Til The White Day is Done*, JLove and Marcella don't get things twisted. In this world of GPS navigation, sometimes a map is the best way to go. Unfold it and get to where we need to be."
--Sacha Jenkins, co-author, ego trip's *Big Book of Racism!* (Regan Books, 2002)

"What would you do if it were your child?" Just one of the multitude of provocative questions and issues raised in this exciting, innovative resource for teachers and trainers. *Love, Race, and Liberation* provides practical, accessible educational tools for use in classrooms and workshop sessions. These ready-to-use lesson plans and compelling personal reflections will challenge learners to awaken their racial consciousness, engage in authentic dialogue about dynamics of race and racism, and develop the critical competencies and commitment to help create inclusive, socially just communities for all people."
--Kathy Obear, social justice educator and advocate, Social Justice Institute (www.sjti.org)

Love, Race, and Liberation

Table of Contents

Introduction

We have both long recognized and long hated that in the United States and much of the world the concept of race makes up a socially constructed reality that dictates, among other things, our overall quality of life. Being "white" often comes with a whole lot of unearned benefits and privileges.

We have both been asked over the years why we make such a fuss about racism. Many people want to know why we care so much. "What's the big deal?" Or, "It's not *your* problem!" "Why are you so sensitive?" So we feel it is important to get clear about the "why," and to do this we need to share a little bit about ourselves.

JLove grew up in an Irish Catholic family in a racially and socio-economically diverse neighborhood in Denver, Colorado. Times got tough when JLove's parents divorced when she was 7 years old. Despite the challenges of raising three kids on her own, JLove's mother never gave up on her faith. Her weekend rituals, instilled and guided by her mom, included putting on their Sunday best and attending their neighborhood church. After Mass, they would take the short drive downtown to help at one of the soup kitchens for the hungry and homeless.

The times she spent at the soup kitchens taught her that we're all in this together and that, all too often, life is not fair. As she stood side by side with her mom and other volunteers dishing out soup, she had plenty of time to count her blessings and wonder if those she served had any blessings to count. Sometimes, children her age peered at her from the other side of the counter, and her discomfort was especially intense. Her young mind could not understand why she had food and a home and the kid in front of her did not. Were they so different?

For Marcella life lessons about racial diversity came in another form. Also born Irish Catholic but in Washington D.C., her parents separated and divorced when she was a baby. Her mother had to work outside of the home because she was a single mom. Marcella's primary caregiver was a Black woman named Miss Wynona. Wynona and her boyfriend, Mr. Robbie, became two very important people in Marcella's already quite complicated young life. Some of Marcella's earliest socialization was vis-a-vis Wynona's extended network of friends and family in the D.C. area. After her second birthday, Marcella and her Mom moved to Ocean City, NJ. While Marcella's mother waited for a new job to start at a local community college, Marcella began school at the local Headstart pre-school. This was also a predominantly African-American space, which continued her unique socialization process regarding race and racial diversity.

After a short time in Ocean City, Marcella's mother met a man/fell in love, remarried /got pregnant, and moved the family to Lindenhurst, New York. The family lived there for a short time, and Marcella attended a few other racially and ethnically diverse pre-schools before they were relocated (based on her step-fathers employment) to South Jersey, specifically a place called Sicklerville, NJ, in Camden County. Marcella attended another racially diverse public school in the early 1980's for Kindergarten and First Grade, and then midway through changed schools again to attend a private school in Vineland, NJ where her mother was a teacher. In her new school she was not a numerical racial or ethnic minority as she had been in other school settings, but in this new school she found out about religious diversity. There was no clear religious majority in the school; there were Muslim, Hindu, and Jewish children, and in fact she was the only Christian girl in her class from first grade to fourth grade. The familiarity with being the "other" or "outsider" because of social identities and being the chronic new girl in class created an acute sense and awareness of "difference" at a very early age. Marcella would again change schools in fifth grade, seventh grade, and tenth grade. In fact, it was not until college that Marcella attended the same school for four years in a row, finally finding a lasting community. These unique experiences were juxtaposed with a U.S. climate that reinforced white privilege and validated white identity, so Marcella was able to notice the injustices and examples of racism and white supremacy first hand.

All of these "unique" experiences and the familiarity with difference that was created through these experiences came to a head in high school. This is when Marcella's choices regarding interracial dating/relationships, the profound connection and solace she had for and with Hip-Hop music and culture, and the beginning of an academic interest in topics such as South African apartheid, biracial/multiracial identity, and social injustice, began to surface. This caused major tension with her parents and often times forced her to compartmentalize circles of friends, as well as her family, in order to navigate what had become a very complex racial terrain. There were many places that she felt comfortable and authentically connected to people, particularly people of color, but this still seemed and felt like a radical way of being in the early 1990s. Marcella observed first-hand that something wasn't right in a system that unfairly advantaged some people but wasn't sure how to talk about it or make meaning of it.

For JLove, high school was also a pivotal time. She entered high school in the late 1980's just as the city implemented a mandatory busing system to desegregate Denver Public Schools. She was bussed to a poor black neighborhood, and the new regulations did the job: her school had kids of all backgrounds, both with regards to race and class. At the soup kitchen she met kids and adults she would never see again. But when she went to high school, she saw kids on a daily basis who were struggling economically. Her classmates had mothers who were single and on welfare. And while there were race-based cliques in the school, there were also real ways to get to know people from other cultures if you chose to take a risk. Some didn't; some did.

JLove is all about her tribe, her clique, her crew, whatever you want to call it; relationships play a huge role in her life. From a young age she found herself riding on the school bus, attending classes, playing sports, going to dances, and just hanging out in communities of color. What she got that kids in the less racially diverse "burbs" didn't get was the opportunity to build intimate, authentic relationships among people from many different backgrounds. Why is this important? When you care about someone, you are invested in his or her happiness and well-being. What happens to that person *affects* you. The bottom line is that at 16 years old, watching one of her best friends get beat down by the cops was different than hearing about some "thug" getting thrown in jail on the six o'clock news.

Contradictions that are inevitable in an unjust system became glaringly obvious to both of us due to authentic and often intimate relationships across racial divides. The importance of these relationships cannot be underestimated and continues today for both of us and fuels our passion and belief that change is necessary and possible. JLove currently lives in Queens, New York, with her husband Hectór Calderón, who is of Dominican descent, and her two biracial sons. Marcella lives in Bed-Stuy Brooklyn with her husband David Hall, a.k.a. DJ Trends, who identifies as Black and of Bajan and St. Kittian ancestry, and they are expecting their first baby.

Both of us live, work, socialize, and are members of multiracial communities, so this work is deeply personal and extremely important. But we know what many of you might be thinking right about now: We are so sick of talking about this race thing. Well, to be honest with you, so are we! Can't we move past this already? Here is the thing, friends, we *can* move past this. There *can* be a day when this "race thing" is behind us. There is just one thing we have to do first: *squash* the racist, white supremacist system that oppresses people of color and that continues to psychologically and spiritually damage all people.

Now please don't get scared when we use that term. We know that some of us, when we hear white supremacy, picture hooded Klansmen riding horses with guns and nooses looking to kill anyone who is black or brown, but white supremacy is much more covert than that. It looks very different nowadays, and that makes it harder to identify and to call it out.

White supremacy is: drug laws that unfairly target poor people; prisons filled disproportionately with black and brown faces; police brutality; lack of equal access to quality healthcare and education; non-white children having higher incidences of asthma because of the polluted air they breathe in run-down neighborhoods; daily assaults on self-esteem via mass media; and perpetual obsession with a "white" standard of beauty. White supremacy has gone undercover.

The bottom line is that in a white supremacist system, one person's life is more valuable than another's, both in the United States and throughout the world. This must change. We are not asking for a higher moral ground here. We are simply asking folks to just be practical about it and to really *think* about it. We really believe that in our heart of hearts, we all know that something is deeply, deeply wrong when we hear about children in this country dying because they have nothing to eat; families that are out on the streets, homelessness during the coldest winter months; and unarmed teenagers shot to death in the back by police. What would you do if that was your child? Would the country turn upside down if two white teenagers were shot by police, because of a case of mistaken identity? Of course we would. The media would go nuts, laws would be changed, and cops would be punished. Why? Because a white person's life is often considered more important than a person of color's life. Just look at the media coverage when a young white women or child is missing; you might think that people of color don't ever get kidnapped in this country, because the media does a good job of underreporting it.

The issues we're exploring together here are just the tip of the frozen white iceberg. There are many more that deserve to be discussed and analyzed, and ideally, some of you, as empowered and inspired educators, will take it upon yourselves to write, talk, and act on the social issues that you are passionate about.

Our hope is that this guide makes you laugh, cry, get angry and indignant, and feel despair but not stay in despair. Our hope is that it helps you reassess your commitment to do what's right, and that we all commit to regaining our humanity.

'Cause no one is free 'til we're all free. Can you get that?

That's why we just can't stop, 'til the white day is done.

Note to Educators

Thank you for supporting this work! We appreciate your commitment to this very important issue and we want to give you some insight into how we hope you will use this book. It is our intention that the 20+ lesson plans and array of love letters will be used in traditional and non-traditional educational spaces. We imagine that the lessons can be used with students as young as 8th grade or as "advanced" as college level. We also believe the lessons can be used in linear order to create an in-depth study of the various issues, thereby creating a comprehensive curriculum, or they can be used as stand-alone lessons to supplement other pieces of your existing curriculum. We also hope you will take advantage of the many innovative extension and interdisciplinary pieces of the lesson plans by creating your own lessons based on the ideas presented. Additionally, we hope that you will make use of all the original works provided by our love letter writers and incorporate their ideas and voices into the work you are already doing. Here a few other additional tips for getting the most out of this book:

1. We believe that race is a social construction; it is not biological or inherent. However because we treat it as if it is real, it means that racism is also very real. Racism exists at the individual, cultural, and institutional levels and we are both conscious and unconscious of how it continues to manifest itself. This should never be left out of analysis or conversation.

2. Definitions are important. Please take note that some lessons provide comprehensive definitions. For the purposes of this book we want to define three important terms from the beginning: Race, Racism, & White Privilege, but realize these definitions are expanded upon in different sections of the book.

   Race: A social construct that artificially divides people into distinct groups based on characteristics such as physical appearance (particularly skin color), ancestral heritage, cultural affiliation or history, ethnic classification, and/or the social, economic, and political needs of a society at a given period of time. Scientists agree that there is no biological or genetic basis for racial categories. (Adams, Bell and Griffin, 2007)

   Racism: A system that unfairly privileges dominant group members on multiple levels, including individually, culturally, and institutionally. This system is based on the social and artificial construction or race.

   White Privilege: Unearned access to resources only readily available to white people as a result of their advantaged social group membership.

3. The title of this book is based on a very important piece of liberation literature by Langston Hughes: the 1926 poem entitled "Dream Variations". Please look for a copy of it, and share with your students so they truly understand the iconic title reference.

4. As we usher in a new era in education under the Obama Administration, we optimistically chose not to include Content Standards References that speak to the No Child Left Behind legislation.

5. While it is not a necessity for using the curriculum, we highly recommend having your organization, school, etc. obtain a copy of the PBS Documentary, *Race: The Power of an Illusion*. It is a life altering resource for teaching about race and ethnicity in the United States. More information available at californianewsreel.org.

6. Please make sure you establish Group Guidelines before you begin having conversations about race and racism. A sample lesson on how to do this is included on page 17.

7. There are many supporting resources created for this book. Please take advantage of them by visiting www.jlovecalderon.com or marcellarhall.com.

8. We want to hear from you! So keep in touch and let us know your thoughts about the book! (love.race.liberation@gmail.com)

9. We believe in the power of education and training and are available to come in and work with your school, organization, etc. (love.race.liberation@gmail.com)

10. Remember that this is part of a larger multimedia project, called 'Til the White Day is Done, which includes an anthology and documentary film. So all of the interviews, quotes, and letters are original works. For more info about this project go to: www.jlovecalderon.com.

Acknowledgments

The editors would like to thank their wonderfully supportive husbands, family, friends, and colleagues!

Special thanks goes to the curriculum writers, the NYU interns, the entire NYU Center for Multicultural Education and Programs staff: Bindi Patel, Laurel Haynes, Mark Carolino, Erica Morales, Adetoro Adegbola and Sarah Meyer. And very special thanks to Allen McFarlane, Assistant Vice-President, Student Diversity and Marc Wais, Vice President of Student Affairs at New York University, for unwavering support of innovative diversity projects like this.

Special thanks to NYU's Center for Multicultural Education & Programs student researchers who are part of the Undergraduate Cultural Training Program: Jordan Budd, Ashley Lekwauwa, and Alexandria Margolis.

And thanks to our dynamite team of women who helped put this together, including the cover art and photography: photographer B-Fresh, make-up artist Angeliq Turner, and graphic designer Caitlin Meissner. Also thanks to Rachel Briggs, our copy editor extraordinaire.

To all of the amazing artists, activists, and cultural icons that agreed to be interviewed-we appreciate you, and our heartfelt thanks goes out to our Love Letter writers for showing how love, vulnerability, and speaking your personal truths are key ingredients of courage.

As mentioned in the Note to Educators, this curriculum guide is one initiative of the multi-media project 'Til the White Day is Done. Many people have generously written, been interviewed, filmed, and otherwise supported the project. A special thanks to all those who have been instrumental in the journey of creating progressive, socially conscious, educational materials to inspire a more just world. Special thanks to: Dr. Jared Ball and his mother Arnette Ball, John Carluccio, Todd Chandler, Jeff Chang, Dr. Perry Greene, Chelsea Gregory, Baba Israel, Corey Kupfer, Talib Kweli, Cameron Levin, Miguel Luciano, M1, Victoria Sanders, Inga Musico, Terrence Nance, Adeeba Rana, Andy Ross, Sonia Sanchez, MC Serch, April Silver, Spacecraft, Kelly Tsai, and Venus.

Sponsors: NYU Center for Multicultural Education and Programs, Eradicating Racism (an initiative of 1+1+1=ONE) and World Up.

The Project: '*Til the White Day is Done* is a holistic journey focusing on white privilege and involving a multi-dimensional and interactive experience through the arts, education, and entertainment. It includes an anthology, the curriculum guide *Love, Race, and Liberation*, edited by JLove Calderón & Marcella Runell Hall, a documentary directed by Byron Hurt and produced by JLove Calderón & Marla Teyolia, and national "town hall" style tour.

And to everyone who came before us, thank you for your courage and commitment.

PART ONE

A Love Letter from Richard A. Chavolla

This is to all my Indigenous sisters and brothers that come from all over the world; my sisters and brothers who have relations, nations, and monumental achievements that precede the European conquests, enslavements, forced laboring; my sisters and brothers who hold memory in their blood, cultural ties, and spiritual connections to lands before they were called the Americas, Africa, or the Pacific Rim.

We wake up each day facing a world that ignores or undervalues our most essential beliefs and actions, but we prevail. We must walk within physical spaces and environments that have been irreconcilably altered. We must often communicate in ways that do not express love, community, cooperation, sharing, respect, and the cyclical nature of the universe just to display what is considered strength and confidence and efficiency and progress. Oh progress, Western progress, that which has brought us to where we are today. Let's really think about its impact on relationships and intimacy and human equity and emotional fulfillment.

We are tempted and forced every moment to consume ideas, images, things, that represent no real connection to our souls, our intellectual history, our eternal bond to our ancestors. In educational institutions we must learn layer upon layer of knowledge and information. First we learn the formal curriculum, then we devise a way to integrate the wisdom of our elders into this curriculum so as to keep our sanity, and then we analytically filter out the racist codes and assumptions imbedded in each and every lesson. In this way we continue to stay close to one another, flourish, learn, resist. When we're young we often sit in classes that are only us, and then if we go on to college, we are often the only one. And then after we leave our formal schooling we dress as we should, talk as we should, operate under the proper worldviews as we should, acknowledge, endure, and sometimes even perpetuate the frequently indifferent or hostile timber of the hierarchy as we should.

And, of course, this just isn't quite enough. We still have eyes and attention avert to others lighter complexioned than ourselves, speaking with that exceedingly comfortable Euro-centric perspective that only comes when it is, in fact, your identity or exhibiting a dozen other subtle traits that make those in power feel good about themselves. Conversely, in other situations, all eyes are upon us, curiously, judgmentally, romantically, as if we speak for an entire population, a population that has been colonized and must explain itself over and over, and then again, may get just one chance. And yes, we do know how to unravel and articulate the mysteries of our oppression if anyone truly cares to listen, but what we know as well is how to demand our liberation, our equality, and our happiness.

So to all my sisters and brothers who keep explaining, who keep demanding, who keep resisting and who keep flourishing, my love goes to you. The world will continue to change and we'll continue to change the world, so as to reflect our lives as we truly wish to lead them.

Richard Chavolla is currently the director of The Center for Multicultural Education and Programs at New York University. Originally from Phoenix, Arizona, he is a long-time educator and advocate for educational equity and opportunities, working at numerous and varied institutions including the American Council on Education, Yale University, Arizona State University, and the Maricopa Community Colleges.

Who Am I? The Question of Identity

Author: Tanesha Barnes

Grades: 8-12+

Suggested Time Allowance: 90 minutes

Materials:
Pens
Personal Identity Wheel handouts
Social Identity Wheel handouts
Newsprint
Markers

Overview: In this lesson students will get to know each other better and learn about the stories of their names. Additionally, students will learn the ways that our social and personal identities impact us as individuals.

Vocabulary: social identity, personal identity, salient

Objectives:
- To provide students with the opportunity to share the stories of their names.
- To introduce students to the terms personal identity, social identity, and salient social identity.
- To reflect on their own personal and social identities and ways that they impact their individual lives.

Activities/Procedures:
1. <u>What is your name story? (35 minutes):</u> Inform students that the purpose of the activity is an opportunity for the group to learn the story about each other's name. Everyone will share the stories of their name and will be given 2-3 minutes to share (with their partner or with the group) Ask the students to answers the questions below when telling the story of their names. You should begin the activity by sharing the story of your name or you can use the sample name story below for artist Talib Kweli.

   Name Story Questions:
   What is the history of your name (first, middle, and/or last)?
   What is the meaning of your name (translation or other meaning as you have learned it)?
   What is the significance of your name? (Are you named for someone or did someone have the responsibility of naming you?)
   If you do not know any of that, share what it feels like to have your name.

"History, Meaning and Significance of Talib Kweli"

"Naming [Talib]…was very deliberate and self-conscious. It was my belief now and it was then that the kind of marginalization and systemic racism that is still present we have allowed and are allowing to be normalized…So what [I] want to do is want both [my] children and the people who meet [my] children to know who they are. And Talib Kweli, generally speaking, means student or searcher of the truth." –*Dr. Perry Greene, Talib's father, in an interview for 'Til the White Day is Done.*

"All my life, teachers had real problems with my name. I remember being told by educators that, with my name, I would never be able to have a real position in America." -*Talib Kweli*

Discussion Questions:
After all students have shared the stories of their name, ask students to reflect and answer the questions below:
1. What is it like to have your name?
2. Does your name reflect anything about your social identities such as your gender, race/ethnicity, sexual orientation, socioeconomic class, or religion?
3. Can people identify you accurately in terms of your social identities based on your name?
4. Do you think people make assumptions about you based on your name?
5. Have you ever felt discriminated against based on your name? Privileged because of your name?
6. Have you ever had to/wanted to change your name? Why?
7. How has reflecting on your name-story impacted you?

Note to Educators: Based on the size of the group and the amount of time available, you can have students share their experience to the group as a whole or in a pair share. For pair share students should be asked to share the stories of their name with another member of the group, preferably someone they may not know very well in the group. Inform the pair that they will have 10 minutes to share their stories and that they will not be interrupted to switch, so they should keep track of time to ensure that both stories are shared. Also inform students that they will not be expected to tell the group the story of the other participants, therefore they do not have to write anything down. They will, however, discuss the experience of sharing their own stories.

Either before or after the Name Story, make sure you take some time to create a safe space by making time for Group Guidelines.

Why are group guidelines important?
Guidelines (rather than "rules") assist facilitators in setting the group tone and in navigating difficult conversations. If for some reason students are not abiding by the guidelines that are agreed upon, the facilitator can refer to the guidelines and agreements hanging on the wall.

Overview: The purpose of this exercise is to make sure that everyone feels that they are participating in a safe space, where their ideas and opinions will be respected. Group Guidelines can set the tone for an entire learning experience.

Objectives:
- To create guidelines for group interactions throughout the lesson.
- To engage students in the process, and hold them accountable to the agreements.

Materials:
Markers
Large sheet of paper

Activities/Procedures:
1. Tell the students that we are going to set up some guidelines for conversation.

2. Ask the students if they have ever created guidelines before and if they know any that they feel are important.

3. Ask the students what things they believe are important to create a safe space.

4. Record the examples on the paper. Be sure to clarify after each statement and ask if the group agrees on it.

5. Examples of sample Guidelines are below:
   - Respect – Sometimes, we may not have the same opinions, but we can still listen respectfully.
   - Confidentiality – Anything of a personal nature that is said here should stay here; theory, ideas, and history should be shared to spread the knowledge!
   - Agree to Disagree – There may be times when the best thing that we can do is agree that we have different opinions.
   - Step (Move) Forward / Step (Move) Back – Try to stay conscious of how much you are participating; if you haven't participated in a while, please step (move) forward; if you have been participating a lot, take a step (move) back.
   - One Mic – One person speaks at a time.
   - Acknowledge power dynamics – Try to stay aware that all of us come from different places and belong to different social identities.
   - Don't make assumptions – Be careful not to make assumptions about fellow participants.
   - Listen for clarity, not debate.
   - Have fun! – This is a place to learn, explore, and have fun.

6. After everyone has contributed, ask if everyone is in agreement with the guidelines on the sheet. When the group has a consensus, pass around a marker as ask the students to 'sign off', tag, or initial the sheet.

Follow up – if you are facilitating the same group for multiple sessions, feel free to remind everyone of the guidelines posted on the wall. You can also type up the guidelines and hand them out at the next session.

2. <u>Personal and Social Identity Wheels (50 minutes)</u>: Distribute a copy of the Personal Identity Wheel to each student. Ask students to take 3-5 minutes to quietly fill in all of the spaces of the Personal Identity Wheel.

Note to Educators: If students ask what is a personal identity or social identity, inform them that the group will come together later to discuss the definitions of personal and social identities.

Personal Identity categories include:
- Political affiliation
- Favorite food(s)
- Favorite music
- Favorite film(s)
- Hobbies
- Talents/Skills/Abilities
- Birth Order
- Other (attribute that is relevant to who you are)
- Favorite book(s)
- Geographic Identification
- Personality Traits

After students have completed their wheel, ask each student to share the category choices from their personal identity wheels with a small group—typically groups of 4-5 are useful for this type of sharing. Following the group share of student's categories, write the term personal identities on newsprint. Ask students to reflect on the categories listed on the personal identity wheel and to collectively define the term personal identities.

Post the newsprint for students to see. Write on the newsprint the various phrases or terms that students present. After 2-4 statements ask the group if they are all in agreement with the definition/words/phrases presented. Then provide students with the complete definition of the term personal identities.

Notes to Educators: Common statements that students present are: personal identities may change from time to time, or personal identities are usually things that we choose.

Personal identities (definition): Individual traits that make up who you are, including your birth order, hobbies, interests, experiences, and personal choices.

Discussion Questions:
1. Did you notice any common themes between or among students in this group?

2. Were there any aspects of your personal identity wheel that you felt especially proud of?
3. Were there any aspects that you felt nervous about sharing?
4. Was it helpful to learn about other people's personal identities? If so, why?

Distribute a copy of the Social Identity Wheel to each student. Ask students to take 3-5 minutes to quietly fill in all of the spaces of the Social Identity Wheel.

Social Identity categories and examples include but are not limited to:
- Race: White, Black, Latin@, Asian/Pacific Islander, Native American, Biracial/Multiracial
- Ethnicity: Anglo, Dutch, African-American, Cuban, Chicano/a, French, Jewish, Lakota, Navajo, Irish, Puerto Rican
- Sexual Orientation: Heterosexual, Bisexual, Lesbian, Gay, Queer, Questioning
- Religion or Spiritual Affiliation: Christian, Jewish, Muslim, Hindu, Bahai'I, Agnostic, Atheist
- Socioeconomic Class: Owning class, upper class, middle class, working class, poor
- Age: Young adult, middle age adult, adolescent, child, senior/elder
- Gender: Man, Woman, Transgender, Gender Queer
- Sex: Male, Female, Intersex
- National Origin: United States, Puerto Rico, Japan, Ireland, Barbados, Dominican Republic
- Physical/psychological/mental/Learning ability: Able bodied, living with a disability, living with chronic disease

After students have completed their wheel ask each student to share the results of their category choices from their social identity wheels with the same small group that they shared their personal identity wheels.

After students have completed the wheel and shared with their group ask students to reflect and answer the questions below:
1. List the identities you think about most often.
2. List the identities you think about the least often.

Following the group share, write the term social identities on newsprint. Ask students to reflect on the categories listed on the social identity wheel and to collectively define the term. Write on the newsprint the various phrases or terms that students present. After 2-4 statements ask the group if they are all in agreement with the definition/words/phrases presented. Then provide students with the complete definition of the term social identities.

Social identities (definition): Primarily group identities, aspects of ourselves where we belong to a particular group. Social identities are shaped by common history, shared experiences, legal and historical decisions, and day-to-day interactions.

Ask students to return their attention back to the social identity wheel because there is one more key term that you would like to present to the group. Write the term **salient** social identity on the newsprint, along with its complete definition.

A **salient** social identity is one that you think about most often and that impacts how you view the world.

Ask students to reflect back on the social identity wheel and the identities that they thought about most often and that others shared as identities they thought of most often. Ask students to the questions below:

1. Why might you think more about some of your group identities than others?
2. What experiences lead you to think so often about the identities that are most salient for you?

Inform students through the course of the above questions that for most people salient social identities are based on areas where individuals feel targeted or oppressed. Also state that most of the time the identities that we think about least are the areas where we have privilege because we don't have to think about them. Examples include: taking public transportation if you are living with a physical disability or having to think about race as a majority person when you are in a placed in situation where you are situationally the "only" one.

Processing Questions:
1. How was it for you doing this activity?
2. Were their any identifiers missing for you?
3. Were there aspects you were nervous about sharing?
4. How are your personal identities connected to your social identities?

3. Take Aways (5 minutes)
Ask students to close out the day's lesson by sharing a take away with the group. (A takeaway is a new insight or idea that they will take with them).

"I grew up inherently nationalistic. I truly believe that any group of people—black, Irish, Russian—you have to work out the problems in your own family. And you can't appreciate somebody else's culture unless you have a full appreciation of your own culture."
–Talib Kweli, interview, 'Til the White Day is Done

Personal Identity Wheel

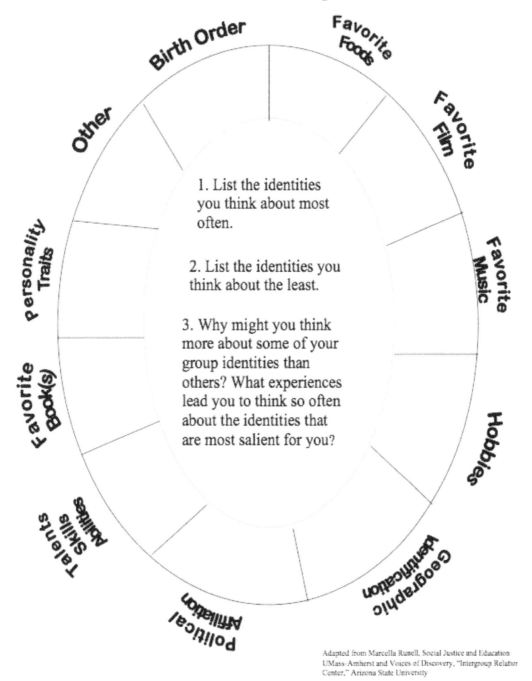

Birth Order

Favorite Foods

Other

Favorite Film

Personality Traits

Favorite Music

Favorite Book(s)

1. List the identities you think about most often.

2. List the identities you think about the least.

3. Why might you think more about some of your group identities than others? What experiences lead you to think so often about the identities that are most salient for you?

Hobbies

Talents Skills Abilities

Geographic Identification

Political Affiliation

Adapted from Marcella Runell, Social Justice and Education UMass-Amherst and Voices of Discovery, "Intergroup Relation Center," Arizona State University

Special Thanks to Ximena Zuniga, and the Intergroup Dialogue Program at University of Massachusetts, Amherst. This lesson plan is adapted from a Gender and Sexuality section created by Davey Shlasko and Marcella R. Hall in Spring 2005.

Social Identity Wheel

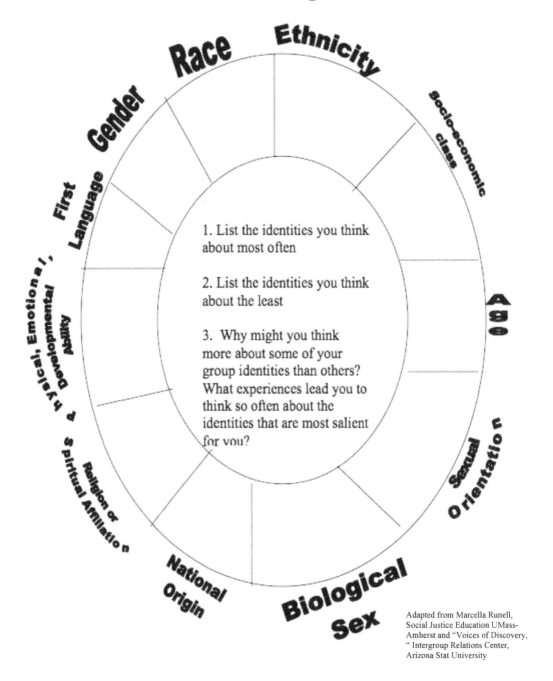

1. List the identities you think about most often

2. List the identities you think about the least

3. Why might you think more about some of your group identities than others? What experiences lead you to think so often about the identities that are most salient for you?

Adapted from Marcella Runell, Social Justice Education UMass-Amherst and "Voices of Discovery, " Intergroup Relations Center, Arizona Stat University

Special Thanks to Ximena Zuniga, and the Intergroup Dialogue Program at University of Massachusetts, Amherst. This lesson plan is adapted from a Gender and Sexuality section created by Davey Shlasko and Marcella R. Hall in Spring 2005.

Social Identity Categories	Examples
Race	White, Black, Latin@, Asian/Pacific Islander, Native American, Biracial, Multiracial
Ethnicity	Anglo, Dutch, African-American, Cuban, Chican@, French, Jewish, Lakota, Navajo, Irish, Puerto Rican
Sexual Orientation	Heterosexual, Bisexual, Lesbian, Gay, Queer, Questioning
Religion or Spiritual Affiliation	Christian, Jewish, Muslim, Hindu, Bahai'I, Agnostic, Atheist
Socioeconomic Class	Owning class, upper class, middle class, working class, poor
Age	Young adult, middle age adult, adolescent, child, senior/elder
Gender	Man, Woman,Transgender, Gender Queer
Sex	Male, Female, Intersex
National Origin	United States, Puerto Rico, Japan, Ireland, Barbados, Dominican Republic
Physical/psychological/mental/ Learning ability	Able bodied, living with a disability, living with chronic disease

Created for WOST 187/Fall 2005/ adapated from Lyon, Catalano, Shlasko & Runell of the School of Education, Social Justice Education

A Love Letter from Julia Ahumada Grob and kahlil almustafa

Black or White: It Don't Matter, It Does

> *"I'm not going to spend my life being a color."*
> - that guy rapping on Michael Jackson's Black or White

On August 28th, 2008, the same day Barack Obama claimed the Democratic nomination, about one hundred and fifty people gathered in New York City on the river's edge between the Brooklyn and Manhattan bridges to help two people cross the threshold of marriage. This potpourri of people, our tribe: dreadlocked, Jewish, Black & Proud, colorful, Chilean, present, mixed ancestry, Japanese, Irish, Egyptian, Canadian, hip-hop, hope-filled, came to witness our wedding. That day we brought to the altar as much of our separate cultural heritages as we could hold in our hands. And we got married.

We are, Julia Ahumada Grob, a daughter of Jewish and Chilean ancestry, and kahlil almustafa, a son of Caribbean, African-American, and Native American ancestry. Our wedding ceremony included the Jewish tradition of Breaking the Glass to seal the covenant of marriage as well as the Jumping of the Broom, a marriage tradition created by enslaved Africans because they were not allowed to marry legally. We also included Tibetan and Yoruba marriage rituals in our ceremony. After our ceremony, a cousin of ours joked that there would be some Inuit Indian people who may feel a little left out because we did not include any of their rituals. Other than that, we had it covered.

Later that day, we danced down the aisle to Michael Jackson's "It Don't Matter if You're Black or White." This song choice reflects our relationship to the conversation of race, acknowledging our racial differences while joyously making fun of it at the same time. Our point was not to say that Race does not matter, just that it should not be the defining factor in human interaction, and still, "yes Race exists." In our case, Race was not a barrier in us choosing to partner during this lifetime.

When we met, we recognized each other as members of New York City's Hip-Hop political activist community. Instantly, we shared a tribal kinship. We both recognized hip-hop activism as rooted in racial justice and as a place where people claim who they are and bring it to the table so we can build together. It is in these multi-racial, multi-ethnic, multi-cultural communities where we both have been able to find home.

Julia Ahumada Grob: *I'm White, but I'm not White, not ethnically White at least. Still I'm a White girl (and a Latina, and a mixed girl) through and through. I am other. Never been pure, never wanted to be. Mostly been accepted as either, all, both, neither. It may be my Yiddishness—a mestizaje of Jewishness, and: Spanish, Austrian, Moorish—the either, all, both, neither.*

kahlil almustafa: *I'm Black but I'm not Black, because I know I have other stuff going on too. My mother didn't raise me along a strict code of Blackness. You're Black so do this or don't do that. Society, the television, history books, random police pat-downs, largely taught me what it meant to be Black. The rest of my Black identity was derived from brave people like my middle school chorus teacher who insisted we sing the Negro National Anthem with pride and the people who wrote books about being Black or who I met in the Reparations movement.*

We both grew up feeling like we did not fully fit in any single world. We both underwent intense personal investigations of racial political conversations. We both see the traditional ways which race is constructed as limiting to how we individually construct our identities. We both look to our family and cultural histories to define how we walk in the world. Now, we build our tribe along shared values, not racial lines.

There are many questions left unanswered. We have not fully explored the extent to which our choice in each other is an expression of our racial beliefs. We also have not figured out what holidays to celebrate. Last year we celebrated Kwanzaakah, marrying our cultural traditions. At this event, we were able to create our own rituals informed from each of separate cultural heritages. This is at the heart of how we approach race during this historical moment. It don't matter, while at the same time, it is what matters most.

Julia Ahumada Grob and kahlil almustafa are both performers, educators, and writers living, breathing, and loving in Brooklyn, NY. This was written on Valentine's Day, 2010, during their second year of marriage.

Understanding the Past to Build a Future: Exploring Racial Socialization

Author: Andrea Dre Domingue

Grades: 8-12+

Suggested Time Allowance: 90 minutes minimum

Subject Areas: Language Arts, Political Science, History

Materials:
Legal-size paper or chart paper
Markers or crayons
Pens

Overview: In this lesson, students will explore the ways in which critical incidents in their lives have influenced their perceptions of their individual racial identity as well as explore issues of race and racism in society at large.

Vocabulary: Socialization, Subordination, Domination, Internalization, Racial Consciousness

Objectives:
- Students will be able to define <u>socialization</u> and <u>consciousness</u>.
- Students will be able to describe how early messages and critical incidents in their lives have socialized them to learn negative beliefs, messages, and behaviors that become internalized as truth in all of us living in oppressive systems.

Evaluation/Assessment:
Students will be evaluated based on written and verbal participation in individual, small group, and large group work as they explore early messages they received about race.

Activities/Procedures:
1. <u>Cycle of Socialization (15 minutes):</u>
   Start by asking students to offer first thoughts or definition about the terms socialization, internalization, and consciousness. General definitions of these terms:
   - **Socialization**: the process of learning norms, beliefs, and practices consciously and unconsciously from individuals, cultures, and institutions about who does and does not have power and privilege as it relates to social categories such as race, gender, sexual orientation, etc.
   - **Internalization**: a process in which those of an oppressed group consciously or unconsciously direct beliefs, practices, norms, etc. held by the dominant group toward one's self.

22

- **Racial Consciousness**: an awareness or recognition of the operation of oppression based on race and how one has a role in maintaining this system. Can also refer to an awareness of one's own racial identity, particularly in how that that identity relates to other racial identities.

Next, introduce the "Cycle of Socialization" model taken from <u>Readings for Diversity and Social Justice, Second Edition,</u> edited by Maurianne Adams, Lee Anne Bell, and Pat Griffin. A brief synopsis of the article is provided below, and a diagram is also available. For more information, please see the supplemental resources section of this lesson.
- *The Beginning:* All individuals are born with no consciousness of social identity, bias, prejudice, or misinformation into a given society that has long operated on a system of oppression.
- *Socialization:* Primary caretakers, who individuals love and trust, begin to influence expectations, norms, values, and roles.
- *Institutional & Cultural:* These early messages are reinforced consciously and unconsciously by institutions (schools, churches, businesses, etc.) and culture (practices, media, etc.)
- *Enforcement:* Individuals who question or challenge these norms are not only enforced to accept the current situation but may also face sanctions or punishment for failing to comply with social expectations.
- *Results:* In response to early process of socialization, individuals may experience a range of emotions and beliefs. Both those who are privileged and oppressed may feel silenced, angry, self-hatred (internalization), guilt, or a sense of hopelessness.
- *Actions:* For this component of the Cycle, individuals must make a choice in how to respond to the systems of oppression and the process of socialization. For many people, they opt to do nothing and allow the system of oppression to stay intact, therefore continually shaping one's identity, beliefs, practices etc. by repeating the previously discussed points in the Cycle.
- *The Core:* At all points of the Cycle individuals are limited or hesitant to take action due to fear, ignorance, confusion, and insecurity. These aspects at the core must be replaced by strength, love, hope, and connection to interrupt the Cycle.
- *Direction for Change:* At this point of the Cycle, individuals have developed an awareness of the system of oppression and one's role in maintaining its operation. Rather than doing nothing, these individuals have made the choice to interrupt the Cycle by raising consciousness, educate others, question, etc.

Note to Educators: Make sure to post a diagram of the model somewhere in the room and/or provide students with handouts of the model. While describing this model, have students give general examples that illustrate the key points of this cycle.

2. Life Mapping (15 minutes):
Place markers/crayons and paper in the centralized location in the room and give students the following instructions:

"Now that we have had an opportunity to get a general understanding of the ways people are socialized in terms of race, we are now going to explore how socialization of race has impacted your life personally. You are to create a map of your life. This map should depict critical messages and incidents that occurred in your life from birth to present day that have influenced your views on race in general and/or your racial identity. Be creative with your map and include as many drawings or words as you feel comfortable displaying."

Note to Educators: Encourage students to spread out within the room and/or find a place that is comfortable for them to reflect and create their life map. It is important to note that students may have difficulty initially creating their map and may need additional time to depict messages and critical incidents. You may want to expand the amount of time for map creation by 5-10 minutes, but remember that this may impact the amount of time allotted for processing this exercise in small or large groups. Also, remind students that this life map is in no way exhaustive and is only being used as a tool to extract particularly significant incidents and messages that may surface when critically reflecting.

3. Small Group Processing (30 minutes):
    Once students have completed their maps, have them break into small groups of 4-5 people. In these groups, students will each share their life map while those in the group listen. The amount of time each person will have will depend on the total time allotted for this section of the activity. It is recommended that students have between 5-7 minutes to share their map without interruptions or questions from the small group. If small groups are not desired or the total number of participants is too small to have small groups of 4-5 students, variations include having students share their life maps in pairs or sharing their maps with the full group.

    Note to Educators: To make sure that each student has an equitable amount of time to share their life map, it is recommended that there is a person delegated to managing time. Students may vary in the detail and time length to which they feel comfortable sharing their life map. Encourage students to use the full amount of time to individually share their map even if that means allowing for moments of silence. Lastly, it is important to encourage students to give their full attention and exercise active listening. As students share their maps, often times those that are listening may be reminded of additional incidents or messages that have influenced their lives. It is suggested to ask students to not make additions to their maps while their peers are speaking.

4. Large Group Processing (30 minutes):
    Once each individual has had an opportunity to share his/her/hir life map, bring students together as a large group and engage them in a conversation about their general experiences during this exercise. Encourage students to draw connects to this activity to the cycle of socialization with particular attention to how messages have been enforced or sanctioned, challenges in interrupting the cycle, and ways in which they have or plan to interrupt the cycle. A listing of suggested questions can be found below.

Interdisciplinary Connections:
English/Literature: Have students write a poem expressing their individual experience developing consciousness about race.

Suggested Processing Questions

- How did it feel to share your life map with others?

- To what extent did you find this activity challenging?

- To what extent did you find this activity to be comfortable?

- What were some early messages that you received about your race or racial identity from your family or peers?

- What were some early messages that you received about races or racial identities different than your own from your family or peers?

- To what extent do these messages relate to internalized subordination and internalized domination?

- Referring back to the "Cycle of Socialization," describe ways in which institutions and cultures enforced or sanctioned messages you received about race?

- What are the potential individual and societal benefits of interrupting the "Cycle of Socialization?"

- What are some reasons why those in privilege may want to maintain this cycle?

- What are some reasons why those of target identities may not take steps to end this cycle?

- Describe any reactions you had to these enforcements or sanctions.

- To what degree have you interrupted the "Cycle of Socialization"?

- Describe any strategies you employ to continually interrupt this cycle.

Supplemental Resources (Optional):

Wijeyesinghe, C.L., Jackson, B.W. (2001). *New perspectives on racial identity development: A theoretical and practical anthology.* New York: New York University Press.

Harro, B. (2000). Cycle of socialization. In M. Adams, et al. (Eds.), *Readings for diversity and social justice* (pp.15-21). New York: Routledge.

Takaki, R. (1993). *Different mirror: History of multicultural America.* Little Brown.

Cycle of Socialization

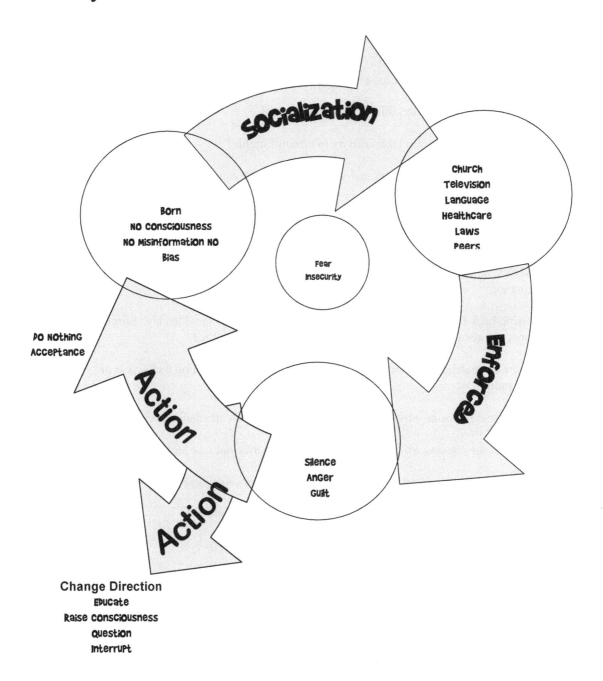

Socialization

Born
NO CONSCIOUSNESS
NO MISINFORMATION NO
BIAS

Church
Television
Language
Healthcare
Laws
Peers

Fear
Insecurity

Enforce

DO NOTHING
ACCEPTANCE

Action

Silence
Anger
Guilt

Action

Change Direction
EDUCATE
Raise CONSCIOUSNESS
Question
Interrupt

*Adapted from Teaching for Diversity and Social Justice, Second Edition (2007).

'I heard it on the news today...'
Exploring the Web of Oppression

Author: Samantha Shapses Wertheim

Grades: 8-12+

Suggested Time Allowance: 120 minutes

Subject Areas: History, Politics, Education, Media

Materials:
Jeopardy game
Markers
Large post-it pads
1 week's worth of different newspapers or printed articles from the internet
Scissors
Scotch tape

Overview: In this lesson students will learn vocabulary words pertinent to discussing the web of oppression and become familiar with the various institutions that contribute to systemic oppression through current events.

Vocabulary: oppression, media, prejudice, discrimination, institutions

Objectives:
- To learn and contextualize vocabulary words pertaining to systems of oppression.
- To discuss the various institutions which participate in the web of oppression
- To use current events to illustrate existing institutional oppression and how they are interconnected in society.

Activities/Procedures:
Pre-work: Students should read 'Discrimination Comes in Many Forms: Individual, Institutional, and Structural' by Fred L. Pincus (15 min)

Note to Educators: If needed this can be read during the class, a PDF version is available at www.jlovecalderon.com

1. Begin the lesson by telling the students that today we will be discussing the web of oppression. Ask the following questions:
   - What did the Pincus article explain to you about oppression and discrimination?
   - What do you think the web of the oppression is? (10 minutes)

2. Definitions –Jeopardy! (50 minutes)

Using the template of the Jeopardy game, students will work together as a team to contextualize the meanings of the words that will help them to discuss the web of oppression. You can create a Jeopardy template at Jeopardylabs.com or you can use paper and hang it on the wall with tape. The grid for the questions is below—please make sure that the questions are facing the wall and that the students can only view the titles and points values (100, 200, or 300)

Racism	Institutional Racism	Institutions	Individual Racism	General –isms
What is a the definition of Racism? 1A	What is Institutional Racism? 2A	What is an institution? 3A	What is individual Racism? 4A	What is an –ism? 5A
Please provide one example of conscious racism. 1B	What is a historical example of Institutional Racism? 2B	Please name 5 institutions that participate in institutional Racism. 3B	Please provide one example of unconscious individual racism and one example of conscious racism. 4B	Please give an example of 5 different –isms. 5B
Please provide one example of unconscious racism. 1C	What is a current example of Institutional Racism? 2C	Please give an example of how two or more institutions work together to support Institutional Racism. 3C	What is the difference between racism and prejudice? 4C	Please give an example of a current law or policy that affects a specific –ism. 5C

Note to Educators: These answers are examples and can be supplemented with alternative, yet accurate answers.
Answers:
Racism
1A: A system of advantage based on race and supported by institutional structures, policies, and practices that create and sustain advantages for the dominant white group while systematically subordinating members of targeted racial groups. This relative advantage for Whites and subordination for people of color is supported by the actions of individuals, cultural norms, and values and the institutional structures and practices of society. (Adams, Bell and Griffin, 2007)
1B: Calling someone a racial slur would be considered conscious racism.
1C: Assuming that a person of color would not be interested in country music.
Institutional Racism

2A: The network of institutional structures, policies, and practices that create advantages and benefits for Whites and discrimination, oppression, and disadvantage for people from targeted racial groups. The advantages created for Whites are often invisible to them or are considered "rights" available to everyone, as opposed to "privileges" awarded to only some individuals and groups. (Adams et. al., 2007)

2B: The institution of slavery is an obvious example of institutional racism perpetuated by the U.S. Government.

2C: Some would argue that No Child Left Behind, by forced closures of underperforming schools, disproportionately affects children in predominantly black and Latino communities.

Institutions

3A: An institution is a particular organizational or methodical operation with established precedent.

3B: Government, Education, Religion, Entertainment, and Judicial Systems.

3C: Through policies enacted by Congress, a part of the US Government, educational facilities and the judicial system unfairly target communities of color.

Individual Racism

4A: The beliefs, attitudes, and actions of individuals that support or perpetuate racism. Individual racism can occur at both unconscious and conscious levels and can be both active and passive. Examples include telling racist jokes, using a racial epithet, or believing in the inherent superiority of whites. (Adams et. al., 2007)

4B: Expecting a person of African descent to be a good dancer is an example of unconscious individual racism. Making a joke about Asians being unable to drive properly is an example of conscious racism.

4C: General –Isms

5A: An -ism is usually used to describe a form of discrimination based on one of the "big seven" societal identities, including race, gender, sexuality, etc.

5B: Racism, sexism, heterosexism, classicism, and ableism.

5C: Don't Ask Don't Tell, a military policy that bans any contribution from homosexual servicepersons.

3. The next exercise will help to contextualize the web of oppression into current events. Write the following words, each on its own large piece of paper, and hang them up on the walls: Education, Criminal Justice System, Labor Market, Religious Institutions, Government / Politics, Media, Banks, Miscellaneous.

4. Ask the students to divide into pairs. Give each pair one or two newspapers, scissors, and tape.

Note to Educators: Feel free to collect articles from other sources. Good sites to visit are
www.cnn.com
www.nytimes.com
www.bbcamerica.com

5. Instruct the students to go through the Newspaper and to pull out any examples of institutional oppression/racism that they can find. The subjects can be illustrations of, predictors of, or related to institutional oppression/racism. (20 minutes)

6. When the students have gone through their new paper, ask them to tape their headlines or articles to the institution that they are related to. (10 minutes)

7. Allow the students to read all of the pages, taking note of the various articles and current events relating to oppression and racism. (5 minutes)

8. Process the sheets with the following questions: (10 minutes)
   - Can anyone recognize any themes on these pages?
   - Are any of these pages related to each other? If yes, how so?

9. Now explain to the students that for the next part we will be making a collage of these current events. Ask the students to pick out the news events that relate to each other and collage them together to create a 'Web of Oppression'
   Note to Educators: depending on the size of the group, students can be divided into two groups. (15 minutes)

10. To process the activity ask the students to summarize the connections between the various news articles and to share any new insights or ideas that they may have had throughout the process. (10 minutes)

Extension Activity: (15 minutes)
Ask students the following questions
   1. What in this collage would have to change in order to create a more equitable society?
   2. What sources can we use to educate ourselves about inequities?

Interdisciplinary Connections:
Civic Engagement: Is there an issue that speaks to you in this collage? What existing policies are there about this issue, and what steps can you take to effect change within these policies or on this issue?

Works Cited

Adams, M., Bell, L. A., & Griffin, P. (2007). *Teaching for diversity and social justice* (2nd ed.). New York: Routledge.

> "White supremacy is racism's agenda manifested, manifested in an ideology."
> --M1, interview, 'Til the White Day is Done

RACE - The Power of an Illusion: The Difference Between Us

Author: Tanesha Barnes

Grades: 8-12+

Suggested Time Allowance: 115 minutes

Subject Areas: Social Studies, Cultural Studies, Ethnic Studies, Sociology, History

Materials:
Pens
Race: The Power of an Illusion film
DVD player
TV
10 *Things Everyone Should Know About Race* worksheet
10 slips of paper with statements

Overview: In this lesson students will learn about the societal construction of race and its lack of biological significance.

Vocabulary: Race, Dominant, Subordinate

Objectives:
- To provide students with the opportunity to explore the construction of race.
- To provide students with the opportunity to explore their own racial stereotypes if it exists.
- To educate students about racism

Activities/Procedures:
1. Warre-Up (10 minutes): Before students arrive, post newsprint or write on a chalkboard "What is Race?" Ask students to respond to this question, while you write the responses. Be sure to differentiate for students that you do not want actual races but the definition of the word race itself.

   Note to Educators: If students give you the definition of race is biological write it; however, underline it or put a star next to it while also letting the students know that you will return to that point later.

   After students have provided you with a list of ideas of the definition for race, write the actual definition as provided below:

Race is not a biological category but an idea, a social construction created to interpret human differences and used to justify socioeconomic arrangements in ways that accrue to the benefit of the dominant social group.

Let students know that the purpose of the today's class is to examine why we think race is all of the things that they described and why it is actually the definition you provided. Also state that you will come back to the definition of race later in the lesson.

2. 10 Things Everyone Should Know About Race Activity (15 minutes): Before the start of the class, write the ten items listed on the 10 Things Everyone Should Know About Race on small slips of paper. Be sure to include the number for each of the statements. To begin the activity, ask the group for ten volunteers. Inform the volunteers that they will have to read the statements on the paper they have selected aloud to the group.

    After all of the volunteers have selected a slip of paper, ask the volunteers to read the statements in order from 1-10, based on the number written on their paper. After all the statements have been read, inform the students that these statements will be the key points that will be covered in the film that they will be viewing today.

    Pass out copies of 10 Things Worksheet and ask students to complete as much of the worksheet as they can base on the information presented in the film with things that fit the ten statements provided.

3. RACE - The Power of an Illusion: The Difference Between Us (60 minutes)

4. 10 Things Worksheet (25 minutes): After viewing the film, ask students to review the worksheet quickly and jot down any last minute notes or ideas that they did not add for the sections provided. Then ask the group to share answers provided for each of the sections, 1-10. As you collect examples from the worksheet about the film, be sure to clarify each of the ten points.

5. Take Aways (5 min): Ask students to close out the day's lesson by sharing a take away with the group. (A takeaway is a new insight or idea that they will take with them).

10 Things Everyone Should Know About Race Worksheet

Instructions: While watching the film, Race: The Power of an Illusion – Part 1: The Difference Between Us, please write any information presented that may be new and interesting to you that fit within the sections provided.

1. Race is a modern idea.

_____

_____

2. Race has no genetic basis.

_____

_____

3. Human subspecies don't exist.

_____

_____

4. Skin color really is only skin deep.

_____

_____

5. Most variation is within, not between, "races."

_____

_____

6. Slavery predates race.

_____

_____

7. Race and freedom evolved together.

_____

_____

8. Race justified social inequalities as natural.

_____

_____

9. Race isn't biological, but racism is still real.

_____

_____

10. Colorblindness will not end racism.

_____

_____

Other information:

_____

_____

_____

RACE - The Power of an Illusion was produced by California Newsreel in association with the Independent Television Service (ITVS). Major funding provided by the Ford Foundation and the Corporation for Public Broadcasting Diversity Fund.

A Love Letter from Dr. Pedro Noguera

A love note to a world free from the burden of race and its micro and macro aggressions

I miss the freedom, the peace, and the ease that comes from being in the majority. I long for the time when I don't have to wonder if the cop who stops to question me, or the woman on the train who clutches her purse, or the cashier who overlooks me when I'm next in line does so not because of my race but because they are simply stupid, afraid, or rude.

Believe me, it makes a difference.

For four years, 1996-2000, I spent my summers in the Caribbean, teaching in Barbados, traveling and doing research in Grenada, Puerto Rico, the DR, Cuba, Trinidad, and Jamaica. After each trip I found myself feeling unusually refreshed and unstressed with lightness in my step, music thumping in my head, and a profound sense of inner peace.

Of course, my sense of inner tranquility never lasted for long. Within a day or two I was back to feeling stressed, rushed, and, too often, irritable. The transformation was impossible to ignore. Part of it was simply my lifestyle. Rushing to appointments, drinking three cups of coffee a day, sleeping four hours a night, all added to my stress and made it necessary for me to walk around with Tums in my pocket to fight off the heart burn I experienced regularly.

But it was more than just my lifestyle and crazy work habits. I realized that I smiled more easily and more readily when I was in the Caribbean and I laughed more too. At first, I attributed the peace I felt to my lighter schedule and the slower pace of life. But as I thought about it I realized that while there I drank coffee (and quite a bit of rum), maintained a full schedule, ate spicy food, and often partied till late at night, I still felt less stress when I was in the Caribbean.

What was it about being in the Caribbean for an extended period of time that left me feeling so chill, so relaxed and so unburdened?

As I thought about it, my mind quickly drifted to the small things: my interactions with the market women in St. Georges, asking for directions from some kids playing stickball on the streets of Habana Vieja, buying coconut water after a soccer game on the Savannah in Port of Spain. Each of these interactions was free of the suspicion and veiled hostility that too often accompanies even mundane conversations in US.

I realized that I was at ease because I was no longer suffering from what Chester Pierce called **MEES**—mundane, extreme, environmental stress. That's the fancy term that he used to describe everyday racism. **Mundane** because it happens all of the time, most often through micro aggressions—small slights, frowns, raised eyebrows, etc. **Extreme** because when a person is bombarded by these kinds of mini assaults it takes a toll and wears away at your sense of humanity and humor. **Environmental** because it's pervasive and almost impossible to escape if you live in the U.S. And **Stress** because all of this induces a considerable amount of stress that we adapt to but it takes a toll on our physical, spiritual, and mental health.

MEES isn't like straight up in your face racism, and it certainly can't be equated with cross burning, lynching, or any of the other gross assaults on our humanity that we endured in the past (and that some still must contend with). But that doesn't mean it's minor or shouldn't be taken seriously. Being bombarded by micro aggressions, institutional racism, police harassment (even when the cops happen to be Black or Latino), takes a toll on you. You only really appreciate it when the burden is lifted and you have the privilege of being yourself.

So this is my love letter to mi Caribe. It's not a love letter written out of naïveté or idealizing the grim realities of the islands. I know that many of my people in the Antilles suffer from underdevelopment, political corruption, hunger, disease, and violence. I know that while the Caribbean may be paradise for North Americans, more often than not it is a site of suffering for us.

Still, I appreciate the benefits of being in the majority and of being among my people with all of their flaws and hang-ups. It's often said that you only appreciate your health when you are sick. Because I live in a sick land, I really appreciate it when I can get a break away.

The Caribbean may not be paradise, and the escape from white supremacy may only be an illusion, but I feel different when I'm there and I love the difference!

Pedro Noguera is the Peter L. Agnew Professor of Education in the Steinhardt School of Culture, Education, and Development at New York University. He also serves as the Director of the Metropolitan Center for Urban Education and the Co-Director of the Institute for the Study of Globalization and Education in Metropolitan Settings (IGEMS). He is the author of several groundbreaking books and has published over 150 research articles, monographs, and reports on topics, such as urban school reform, conditions that promote student achievement, youth violence, and race and ethnic relations in American society.

Race Isn't Biological, but Racism is Still Real.

Author: Tanesha Barnes

Grades: 8-12+

Suggested Time Allowance: 90 minutes

Subject Areas: History

Materials:
Newsprint
Markers

Overview: In this lesson students will discuss the significance that race plays in our society.

Vocabulary: Colorblind, Systemic

Objectives:
- To provide students with the opportunity to discuss the effects of stereotypes and race.
- Explore the advantage and disadvantage of a colorblind society.

Activities/Procedures:
1. <u>Warm-Up: (15 minutes)</u>: Write the definition for the word race on newsprint or on the chalkboard for students to see as they enter the room. Keep this definition in view throughout the entire lesson. Ask students to reflect on the Race: The Power of an Illusion film and to take 5 minutes to write the main ideas or points that they remember learning from the film. Ask students to share what they have written with the larger group.

2. <u>Fishbowl Activity (75 minutes)</u>:
   Note to Educators: This activity requires a room with chairs that are moveable. Based on the number of students in the group, break them up into three smaller groups ensuring that the groups are no bigger than ten people. Explain to students that each of the three groups will be given the opportunity to discuss being in the fishbowl. Being the fishbowl means that they will have to sit in the middle of the room in a circle in their small group discussion the question provided for them. They will be given ten minutes to talk as a group, at which time the students outside of the circle/fishbowl will have to be quiet and listen. For each other of the groups, ask one student to volunteer to be the moderator. Explain that as the moderator, the student will be responsible for posing the questions to the group, continuing the conversation in the group when necessary and they must take part in the conversation as well.

   Provide each of the groups with the one or more of the questions below to discuss while in the fishbowl:

1. Since we have now learned from the film, Race: The Power of an Illusion, that race is not biological, why do you think that race and racism still exist in our society?

2. Discuss the statement below by M1 in an interview for 'Til the White Day is Done, a member of the hip-hop duo Dead Prez:

"What I recognize racism as, from my political education, is a byproduct of this greater system that has been fashioned in order to exploit African labor. In specific, it is the system that was supported by Europe and North America that helped create this whole American stronghold that we have today, which came into power as a result of bondage. You know the free and damn near free labor of Africans and everybody else at their expense. So in order to hold the colonies in place and to preserve the notion that what was happening was correct, they had to create the idea that it was ordained by a greater spiritual thing and that the people involved in it were inferior."

3. At the end of the film, it is revealed that Gorgeous is both a star athlete and a valedictorian. Did you have any initial reacts to this statement? Where you surprised? Does it meet the stereotypes that we would have of someone like Gorgeous?

4. Discuss the statement: colorblindness will not end racism. Do you believe that we can exist in a colorblind society? What are advantages and disadvantages to someone adopting a colorblind ideology in our society?

After all groups have had the opportunity to be in the fishbowl, ask students to return to their original seats. Inform students that we will now discuss the process of taking part in the fishbowl activity.

Processing Questions:
1. What are your initial thoughts on the fishbowl activity?
2. What was it like being inside of the fishbowl?
3. What was it like to be outside of the fishbowl listening in?
4. Where there moments when you the group inside the fishbowl discuss something that you wanted to comment on or react to? If yes, what was said and what is your comment?

3. Take Aways (5 minutes): Ask students to close out the day's lesson by sharing a take away with the group. (A takeaway is a new insight or idea that they will take with them).

Race, the Power of an Illusion:
The Story We Tell

Author: Samantha Shapses Wertheim

Grades: 8-12+

Suggested Time Allowance: 120 minutes with full version; 90 Minutes with abridged version

Subject Areas: History

Materials:
Race the Power of and Illusion Film, part II
Race the Power of an Illusion ditto
Large post-it pad or blackboard
Markers

Overview: This lesson will use the film Race, the Power of and Illusion to discuss the discrepancies of what students have learned in school versus the realities of the creation of race in American society.

Objectives:
*   To reflect on what students have learned about the creation of race in the United States.
*   To share historical information provided by the film Race the Power of an Illusion.
*   To empower students to look for new ways of educating themselves about United States History.

Activities/Procedures:
1. Before the students arrive write a definition of race on the board and write the following topics on large paper hung around the room: Declaration of Independence, Thomas Jefferson, Labor/Slave Trade, American Indians/Western Expansion, Andrew Jackson, American Indian Removal Act, Science in the 19th Century, Abolition and Slavery, Dred Scott, White Man's Burden/Philippines, The World's Fair.

    Race: A social construct that artificially divides people into distinct groups based on characteristics, such as physical appearance (particularly skin color), ancestral heritage, cultural affiliation or history, ethnic classification, and/or the social, economic, and political needs of a society at a given period of time. Scientists agree that there is no biological or genetic basis for racial categories. (Adams, Bell and Griffin, 2007)

2. To begin the lesson, state the goals: Today we will be watching Race, the Power of and Illusion Part II, to learn more about the creation of race in American history.

3. Provide every student with a marker and ask them to walk around the room and write down what they have learned in the past about these subjects. Let the students know that if they do not know anything about the subject, they can skip the page. (15 minutes)
4. Allow the students time to walk around and read what others have written. (5 minutes)
5. As a group, summarize each sheet. (5 minutes)
6. Pass out the following ditto, and instruct the students that they should fill out the ditto as they watch the film. (34 minutes abridged version, 56 minutes regular version)

Subject/Person	What I already knew	What I am learning right now
Declaration of Independence		
Thomas Jefferson		
Labor/Slave Trade		
American Indians/ Western Expansion		
Andrew Jackson		

American Indian Removal Act		
Science in the 19th Century		
Abolition and Slavery		
Dred Scott		
White Man's Burden		
The World's Fair		

7. When the film has finished ask the students to share with the group the differences between what they knew and what they learned. Ask the following questions: (20 minutes)

- When did you learn about these topics?
- What resources did you learn from?
- What surprised you about this film?
- What didn't surprise you?

Extension Activity: (20 minutes)
Personal Share: Have the students to break up into groups of 2 or 3 people and ask them to share with their partners what their experience learning history/social studies has been thus far.
- What topics did you learn about?
- Who was your best history/social studies teacher and why?
- What types of books did you read in your history/social studies classes?
- Do you think that you learned everything that you wanted to know?
- What can you do about it? What action steps can you take in your particular community?

---

8. Liberate: group brainstorm bubble (20 minutes)
On the board or newsprint/chart paper draw a bubble and put a topic inside of it, such as Native Americans and Western Expansion. Ask students to volunteer to come up to the board and draw a bubble off of your bubble that includes a way to learn more or explore this issue. Students can draw as many or as few 'brainstorm bubbles' as they like. Bubbles can be underlined for emphasis and can spring off of one another. At the end of the exercise, have the students write down the bubbles that strongly resonate for them as future areas of research and exploration.

Interdisciplinary Connections:
Literature: Memoirs are a great way to learn about history from a personal perspective. As an assignment ask the students to choose and read a memoir from a historical figure.

Works Cited
Adams, M., Bell, L. A., & Griffin, P. (2007). *Teaching for diversity and social justice* (2nd ed.). New York: Routledge.

Express Yourself:
Processing Privilege Through the Arts

Author: Samantha Shapses Wertheim

Grades: 8-12+

Suggested Time Allowance: 90 minutes

Subject Areas: Language Arts, Fine Arts

Materials:
Notebook/journal
Blank white paper
Pens
Classroom board or hand out
Quotes or clips from *'Til the White Day is Done*
Markers, crayons, additional art supplies

Overview: In this lesson, students will use quotes or clips from JLove Calderon's 'Til the White Day is Done project to inspire journaling, poetry, and artistic expression. This lesson will assist students in processing the information given to them, and will open up opportunities for sharing among group members.

Vocabulary: Free write, Haiku, Abstract Art, Journaling

Objective:
- To expose students to expressing themselves through different artistic mediums.
- To encourage students to reflect on privilege through writing and art.
- To assist students in processing information given to them from 'Til the White Day is Done.

Activities/Procedures:
1. Begin with the goals of the exercise: This exercise will assist you in processing information regarding privilege in a variety of different ways. We are going to explore different methods of artistic expression using free writing, journaling, poetry, and abstract art. (10 minutes)

   Pass out the page with suggested quotes or show the clips from 'Til the White Day is Done'

   Suggested quotes:

   "The original sin is slavery, and my ancestors were part of that, and I benefit from racism, white privilege and white supremacy every single day that I draw breath"
   -JLove Calderon

"It was in junior high school where cops went from being people who looked like they could help you, to them looking at me with suspicion. I remember that feeling. All through my life, teachers had real problems with my name. I remember being told by educators that, with my name, I would never be able to have a real position in America. I remember people telling me, when I had my first son, named Amani Fela, that I shouldn't have named him an African name because he could never be president with an African name."
-Talib Kweli

"As long as in places, like New York City, there's 50% unemployment among Black men, where Black children still die at twice the rate at birth as white children; as long as in some parts of the country where there are Black and Latino children who remain two or three years behind their white counterparts; as long as there are people directed into what communities they can and cannot live in and what loans they can get and what small business protection they get; as long as there are Katrinas, as long as we are willing to suspend the rights of young Black men in the streets all across America just because they're young, Black men."
- Dr. Perry Greene

"What I recognize racism as, from my political education, is a byproduct of this greater system that has been fashioned in order to exploit African labor. In specific, it is the system that was supported by Europe and North America that helped create this whole American stronghold that we have today, which came into power as a result of bondage."
-M1

"Most of the time, when you hear white privilege, we think of rich people, and we think of people who run institutions. We think of old money, old wealth and that's not to say that's a mistake, and that white privilege doesn't exist in any of those areas I just mentioned. But when I think of white privilege what's really on my mind today is…white Obama voters. And white Obama supporters. Particularly white Obama supporters who left where they were from in the United States and moved to California, Illinois, and New York. I feel that no matter how progressive white folks think we are, and no matter what kind of work we do— even if we're teachers and we're activists or community organizers—we still are unaware of our own white privilege in our everyday lives because we have identified the enemy as older, rich white people."
- Danny Hoch

Instruct the students to choose one quote that resonates strongly with them to focus on for the entirety of this exercise.

2. Free Write (10 minutes)
Write the term Free Write on the board, and ask the students if they can give you an explanation of what the term means.
After the students have finished, summarize:
Free Write is to write without restrictions; it can make as much sense or as little sense as you want. It can consist of words, phrases, or sentences. The only thing that matters with Free

Writing is that you are writing. Free writing does not have to be shared with an audience; free writing can be just for you.

Instruct students to take out the journals or paper and 'Free Write' for 5 minutes about their chosen quote. They must write for the entire 5 minutes, even if they choose to simply repeat what they have already said.

3. Journaling (15 minutes)

   Write the term Journaling on the board, and ask the students if they have any idea how this might differ from free writing?

   After the students have contributed explain to them that like free writing, journals can be kept private, information that you get to choose if and when you want to share it. However, journals are usually more structured. Therefore the next exercise will be more structured. The student's will now have 10 minutes to answer the following questions:

   - What facts do you know regarding this quote?
   - What feelings do you have regarding these facts?
   - How do these feelings affect your actions?

4. Poetry (20 minutes)

   In order to encourage the use of poetry we will be using the format of a Haiku. Haikus provide a bit more structure to write poetry. Write the term Haiku on the board, and ask the students if they know what a Haiku is. After the students have contributed share with them that Haiku is one of the most important forms of traditional Japanese poetry. Haiku is, today, a 17-syllable poem. The first line contains 5 syllables, the second like contains 7 syllables and the third line contains 5 syllables. Haiku's have the ability to create simplicity out of complicated emotions, events, or descriptions. (Toyomasu, 2001)

   Haiku example:

   complicated thoughts
   swelling around privilege
   overwhelm my head

   Steps to writing a haiku:
   1) Think of the title based on your quote
   2) Start to write down words you associate with the title
   3) Place words into lines, and count out syllables.

   Give students 15 minutes to create their Haiku.

   When finished students can share their haikus with the class at the end of this exercise, or you can post them on the walls later (anonymously) for all students to read.

5. Abstract Art (25 minutes)

   Write the term Abstract Art on the board. Ask the students if they know what abstract art is.

After they have contributed explain that in many ways abstract art is very similar to free writing; there are no rules. It is simply an expression of what they are feeling. Abstract art does not have to 'look' like anything. It is a collection of shapes and forms that come together to create a picture.

Now we will be creating an abstract art piece based on the quote you have chosen, your free write, journal entry, and haiku.

Ask the students to close their eyes and ask them the following questions: (20 minutes)

What colors are your quote?
What shape is it? Is it jagged? Is it soft?
What is the pattern of your quote? Is it busy? Is it calm?
What is the size of your quote? It is a large picture, is it detailed?

Using the vision in your head, please take the art supplies and begin to draw about the quote you chose. Use your free write, journal entry, and haiku to inspire you. You can include images, words, and colors—anything that you feel expresses yourself.

Afterwards, the drawings can be hung up to create a gallery space that the students can view. You can hang the haiku's with the pictures as well. (5 minutes)

6. Conclusion (10 minutes)
   Ask the students the following questions to process and end the exercise:
   Which of these activities was the most difficult for you? Why?
   Which activity was the easiest? Why?
   Are there any 'take aways' that people would like to share?

Interdisciplinary Connections:
History: Free writing can also be used as a tool to explore historical events and historical figures. You can reframe this lesson by choosing different quotes from historical figures and events. Good resources for video clips or quotes can be found at:
http://www.peopleshistory.us/watch/videos
http://www.quotationspage.com/

Works Cited
Toyomasu, K. G. (2001, January 10). *Haiku for people*. Retrieved from
    http://www.toyomasu.com/haiku/#whatishaiku

A Love Letter from Sofia Quintero:
A Love Letter to White Allies in the Struggle for Racial Justice

I can only imagine what you were expecting, but I'm pretty sure it wasn't this.

You've shown up to every meeting. You're mindful of how much space you take except to be the first to call out anything that the remotest odor of racism. You laugh at the "white people" comments, your own barbs at the most egregious and deserving targets ranking among the funniest.

And then it happened.

You said one thing or did another, and now everyone looks at you differently. You didn't mean anything by it. You're so ready to make things right, but it seems the harder your attempts, the worst it gets. That's not *you*, you insist. Still with one small act, the trust seems to have been irrevocably broken. In fact, the good will was so easily shattered, you start to question if it were ever there.

You go from embarrassed to hurt to angry (although that you keep to yourself.) You feel set up. You want to yell, "I've been bamboozled!" but you know *that'll* just get you into more trouble and so you don't. You don't think you'll ever speak freely in mixed company again. You wonder if you should just walk away and take on another cause.

This is what racism has wrought.

You may not believe this, but some of us do stand up for you. We knew this day would come—it always does—and we have learned that this is par for the course in the quest for racial justice. It's not that we aren't hurt or angry by what you said or did. We just get that this is what it means to have multiracial alliances.
If we have our way, we will mine the conflict for opportunities to deepen the connection we have with you.
But as you can see, it's extremely difficult to convince the others that sometimes a White person has earned the right to be struggled with and that struggle is part of building movement and creating change.

I write this love letter to see if I can make you understand why it is so difficult. Have you ever seen the film *The Mirror of Privilege: Making Whiteness Visible?* In that documentary, a White woman says that she "got" it when an African American woman explained the difference between the way White Folks and People of Color approach the possibility of interracial friendship. She said that when a White person wants to be friends with a Black person, all she has to do is walk across the room, extend her hand and introduce herself. When a Black person makes that decision—and I'm paraphrasing here—she is crawling across the room across the shards of broken relationships with White people in the past. Ain't no way to start a friendship, is it?

But this is what racism has wrought.

You cannot imagine how many times, for example, women of color have had White women shut down a conversation about race under the guise of focusing on "*all* women?" How often have White people in the media advanced their careers telling stories about People of Color, making it almost impossible for us to produce our own narratives? Do you know how many times organizing groups headed by well-meaning White leaders have parachuted into our communities and then almost instantaneously commanded all the funding as if organizations with indigenous leadership and in need of resources did not already exist in those neighborhoods? If you were to pick up any of the shards of which that African American woman spoke, these are just three of the million reflections you would see.

I know. You *have* seen some of these things. You might have even spoken out against them. And, no, it is not only your responsibility alone to address them. You are only one person, and we are supposed to do it together. That is precisely why you showed up in the first place.

But you must grasp just how outnumbered you are. We have come to value you so much that we venture out in search of more of your kind only to have our hearts broken. What you are going through right now happens to us all the time. Do you know how many times we were made to feel safe in a predominantly White space to be alienated once we brought up anything about race? Do you know how pervasive "color-blind racism" has become? (Once you've watched *Mirrors of Privilege*, cop Eduardo Bonilla-Silva's *Racism Without Racist*s.) Do you know how what the average White person does when that dialogue ceases to be about *other* faceless White people of the past and focuses specifically on she or he benefits from what those people did to this very day?

She packs up her privilege and leaves. The ability to trump one's Whiteness with some other identity—"I'm a woman, I'm working-class, I'm a good person, etc."—all without giving up the spoils of supremacy is perhaps the biggest privilege of Whiteness of all. Ironic, isn't it?

And this is why we seek to separate whether it is creating our own organization or claiming our own table. We *need* to separate sometimes for our own welfare. And so when we meet folks like you and take the risk to integrate our spaces, even the most honest of mistakes can feel like hammering open a cast before the bone has fully healed. And if the mistake seems less than honest …

I know. No one wants to have his goodness called into question. Least of all when all he did was be imperfect. Especially when unlike others of the same privilege, he has chosen to step up for change. Trust me, I get it. As a heterosexual ally for queer liberation, I've been there. I know some men involved in feminist movement who have been there, too. We can go down the identity checklist and draw parallels all day long, but I hope you understand that herein lies the rub.

Because of what racism has wrought, this is what it means to be an ally.

I cannot tell you whether you should stay or go. You may not even have a choice in the matter. But if you do, I encourage you to ask yourself, "Am I just picking up my privilege and walking away?" At the heart of that question is what it means to be an ally. An ally sits in the fire that we cannot easily flee. And you know what? That includes those occasional fires that—for whatever reasons—we may have set ourselves.

How about it I make a deal with you? You have my word that some of us will continue to advocate for your essential goodness. We will take on the discomfort that ensues when we point out the dissonance between demanding that White people be allies only to show them the door the second they reveal themselves to be human. We will remind our kin that you are not there to save us but to liberate yourself, and that it is not acceptable for us to take out on you our rage at other White people. We will raise the painful question of just how effective we are being in empowering ourselves if we remain so easily threatened by the few White bodies in the room.

In return, I ask you to separate your intentions from your impact and to be willing to be accountable for what you say and do. I request you expand your contribution to racial justice to include your building with other likeminded White folks and finding the courage to discuss White privilege with those who deny that it exists. I caution you to attend to your guilt because it has counterproductive tendency to hear things that were never said, serving no one, least of all you.

Most of all, if we are truly in this together and you want me to go to bat for you when your fallibility makes you seem too much like the racists they have encountered before, the last thing you should do is pack up your privilege and leave.

Sofia Quintero is the President of Sister Outsider Entertainment and the co-founder of Chica Luna Productions. She is the author of several novels across genres including the feminist hip-hop noir which she writes under the pen name Black Artemis. Her latest is the young adult novel Efrain's Secret (Knopf 2010.) As a filmmaker Sofia wrote and co-produced the short film Corporate Dawgz, a comedic ode to White people who "get" it. To learn more about Sofia and her work, visit www.blackartemis.com.

Ain't I an American? Exploring United States Immigration History & Citizenship

Author: Andrea Dre Domingue

Grades: 8-12+

Suggested Time Allowance: 90 minutes minimum

Subject Areas: History, Language Arts

Materials:
Chart paper
Markers
Sticky Notes (if possible 4 different colors)
Pens
Race: Power of an Illusion DVD or VHS

Overview: The goal of this lesson is have students explore the collective histories of how various racial and ethnic groups immigrated into the United States and how these patterns relate to construction of citizenship and whiteness.

Vocabulary: Immigration, Citizenship, Naturalization, Melting Pot

Objectives:
- Students will be able to describe the social construction of citizenship and how it has influenced the degree to which racial groups have had access to power and resources within the United States.
- Students will be able to identify examples of how the historical legacy of immigration has shaped their personal experiences or the experiences of their family.

Evaluation/Assessment
Students will be evaluated based on their participation in group activities and discussion as well as their critical analysis of the film excerpt.

Activities/Procedures:
1. Warm-up Activity (30 minutes):
   Distribute packs of sticky notes and pens, and ask participants to take several notes and a pen. Post several sheets of chart paper in the room and title the sheets with the terms "Immigration," "Citizenship," "Naturalization," and "Melting Pot." Instruct students that they are to use the sticky notes and pens to write down any initial thoughts that come to mind about the terms posted on the chart paper. Inform students that these thoughts can be actual beliefs they hold, messages they received from others or media, stereotypes, questions they may have, etc.

Once students have had a chance to write their thoughts, have them post the stick notes on the chart paper. Have volunteers read the notes posted on each sheet, and ask the group to first collectively create a definition and identify any themes about each term. If necessary offer definitions for these terms if they have difficulty.

Note to Educators: Since there are several terms in which the students have to respond to, it is suggested that each term is assigned a different sticky note color if possible, or have students respond to each term one at a time to avoid confusion. It may be also helpful to introduce one sheet at a time so that students can focus on a given term without distraction from the other terms.

2. Race Power of Illusion (30 minutes):
   Show Episode 3 of *Race: The Power of an Illusion: The House We Live In,* cueing the film from the beginning of this episode until 26:28. Encourage students to pay particular attention into issues of immigration, citizenship, naturalization, and the melting pot as previously explored.

3. Group Processing (30 minutes):
   At the conclusion of the film screening, engage students in an Agree/Disagree continuum activity. Post the word "Agree" one side of the room and the word "Disagree" on the other. Inform students that a series of statements will be read and they are to move along the continuum in the room to the extent in which the statement is applicable to their personal experiences.

   Following this activity, have students participate in a discussion processing the continuum and the film. Suggested questions are below:

   - What types of challenges might your ancestors faced when migrating?
   - In what ways might your ancestors have had access to resources, job, land, etc.?
   - What are some reasons as to why people immigrated to the U.S.? How have these reasons stayed the same or changed over the years?
   - Bonilla-Silva argues that some people did not have access to be a part of the melting pot and that in fact people of color were not included and in some regards served as tools or supplies to create or heat the pot. What does he mean by this statement? What is your personal reaction to this statement? To what extent has the elements of what is used to create and sustain the melting pot changed or remained the same?
   - A central argument in the film is that whiteness was socially constructed and in many instances became synonymous with citizenship, power, and privilege in U.S. How has the concept of whiteness and citizenship changed over time?
   - In what ways did the film relate to the experiences that your family or you personally have had? In what ways were your family experiences different?
   - What are the contemporary effects of immigration?
   - Have the collective experiences of people of color changed or stayed the same in regards to access to citizenship and participation in society since pre-World War II?

Extension Activities:

1. For homework prior to this lesson assign students the task of investigating their family's immigration history into the United States. This can be done by simply having students ask their immediate caretakers or extended family about what they know about their immigration history. This activity can also be done as a homework assignment after the lesson which they can write a reflection paper of this information in relation to what was learned from the lesson's activity and film.

2. For a visual activity, post large maps of the United States, world, and state/region in which you reside. Have students plot where their immediate family and two to three generations earlier have predominantly resided. After plotting, lead student sin a discussion about themes identified while also exploring why students may have had difficulty or ease in identifying this family history.

Interdisciplinary Connections:

Creative Writing: Have students write a poem or fictional short story describing how his/her/hir family arrived to the United States.

Supplemental Resources (Optional):

Olsen, L. (1998). *Made in America: Immigrant students in our public schools*. New York: The New Press.

Roediger, D. R. (2005). Working toward whiteness: *How America's immigrants became white: The strange journey from Ellis Island to the suburbs*, New York: Basic Books.

Agree/Disagree Activity

1. I have changed or altered my name so that others would have less difficulty writing it.

2. I have changed or altered the pronunciation of my name to so that others would have less difficulty saying it.

3. I have difficulty finding local businesses that offer products or services for my racial or ethnic identity.

4. I have felt pressure to assimilate or compromise my racial or ethnic identity.

5. I am knowledgeable about my family's immigration history.

6. I feel that I can easily trace my family's immigration history through public records.

7. I have family members who currently live outside of the United States.

8. I feel like I am an American citizen or have close ties to the United States.

9. I had to learn to speak or write English at some point in my life.

10. Most of my family lives in my birth country.

11. I find visiting my birth country accessible.

12. I have the ability to travel outside of the United States without difficulty.

13. My ancestors had the legal and financial resources to own property.

*Adapted in part from "Common Ground" in Teaching for Diversity and Social Justice, Second Edition (2007).

"The House We Live In" Unpacking the Impacts of Racial Oppression on Housing

Author: Andrea Dre Domingue

Grades: 8-12+

Suggested Time Allowance: 120 minutes minimum

Subject Areas: History, Language Arts

Materials:
Copies of "Oppression: Levels & Types Worksheet"
Pens
Chart Paper
Markers
Race: Power of an Illusion DVD or VHS

Overview: The goal of this lesson is have students explore the different levels and ways that oppression manifests in society through the lens of race and the development of the suburbs. The film *Race: Power of an Illusion* will serve as introduction to these manifestations where students will conclude the session by participating in a fishbowl activity to process observations from the film and personal experiences.

Vocabulary: Suburbia, red lining, wealth, net worth, urban renewal

Objectives:
- Students will be able to describe the factors that influenced the development of the suburbs.
- Students will be able to define levels and types of oppression.
- Students will be able to identify examples of oppression through the lens of housing and race.

Evaluation/Assessment:
Students will be evaluated based on their critical thinking skills through completion of the "Levels and Types of Oppression Worksheet," as well as their verbal and active listening skills through their participation in the fishbowl group activity.

Activities/Procedures:
1. Levels & Types of Oppression (10 minutes):
   Introduce the "Levels and Types of Oppression" model taken from Teachings for Diversity and Social Justice, Second Edition Edited by Maurianne Adams, Lee Anne Bell, and Pat

Griffin. A brief synopsis of the model is provided below. For more information, please see the supplemental resources section of this lesson.

- Ask students to recall the definition of oppression. For definitions, please see Lesson 3 in this book.
- Have students generate a list of examples of oppression as it relates to race and write these examples on chart paper with markers.
- Inform students that oppression is manifested in society at three levels: individual, cultural, and institutional levels. Have students generate definitions of these levels based on their understanding of oppression and identify examples of these levels using what was written on the chart for assistance.
  - *Individual*: behaviors or attitudes held about a group that directly impacts an individual.
  - *Cultural*: refers to norms, practices, beliefs, roles, etc. held collectively that views a group as inferior.
  - *Institution*: deeply rooted, policies, laws, and customs by organizations of societal institutions (government, education, law, healthcare, etc.) that systematic disadvantage a particular group.
- In addition to these levels, oppression can manifest consciously or unconsciously. For a further explanation of consciousness, please refer to lesson #1 of this book. Have students generate examples of unconscious and conscious instances of oppression.

2. Race Power of Illusion (30 minutes):
Show Episode 3 of *Race: The Power of an Illusion: The House We Live In"*, cueing the film from 26:28 until the end of the episode (approximately 30 minutes). While students are watching the film, have them complete the "Oppression: Levels & Types Worksheet," instructing them that they are to write examples of oppression that they observe from the film.

3. Fishbowl Activity (80 minutes):
At the conclusion of the screening, have students free write any reactions they had from the film for about five minutes. Next instruct the group that they will be moving into caucus groups based on race. People of color will be in one group and white students will be in another. Inform students that each group will have approximately 20 minutes to discuss any immediate reactions to the film as well as having a chance to discuss distinct experiences people of color and white people may have with different levels and types of oppression.

Note to Educators: While the above Fishbowl has students arrange themselves in caucus groups based on race, other social identities such as social class and nationality status could also be used.

Caucus Groups (40 minutes):
Have students get into caucus group based on race, stressing that they are to self-select which group they are to participate in based on the identities that they are most connected to. The groups should have some distance between them so that students can speak freely without the other group being able to hear what is being shared. Instruct students that they will have an

opportunity to discuss their immediate reactions to the film screening, to share any examples of oppression identified on their worksheets, and to speak generally about issues of race, housing, and levels of oppression through the lens of their racial identity. It s suggested that there are facilitators who share the group's social identity to work with each caucus group to help students engage in a conversation. If there are not enough facilitators for this, ask for a student to serve in this capacity while lead facilitator(s) move between each groups observing the conversation.

Note to Educators: It is important to remind students that they are to self-select which caucus group they will participate and feel most connected to. This is particularly important for those students who may identify as multiracial. Some multiracial students may have a hard time deciding which group they will join and in some instances if there is a critical mass, may even request to form a multiracial caucus group. If this is the case it is suggested to support students in creating an additional caucus group.

After students have moved to their respective groups, on flip chart paper post some discussion questions for each group to respond to. Suggested questions are below:

Suggested questions:
• How does it feel to be identified in this group?
• What are some advantages and disadvantages of being a member of this group?
• What are your immediate reactions to the film?
• In what ways have instances of oppression impacted you or your family, particularly in regards to where you grew up?
• What experiences have you had with racism on the individual or cultural level?
• Are there any questions you would like to ask the other caucus group(s), if yes what questions?

Fishbowls (20 minutes):
 Arrange the seating in the room to form two concentric circles and re-post questions that were posed in the caucus group. When the caucus groups have concluded tell students that they are now going to move into an activity where each caucus group will have a chance to discuss highlight of their conversations (inner circle) while the other caucus group observes (outer circle). It is important to stress to the groups that when they are in the outer circle, they are not ask any questions, make any comments, and should observe using active listening skills. While in the inner circle, these students are to speak freely about their experiences in the caucus group. It is suggested that each facilitator for the caucus groups participates in the inner circle and assist the groups in having a conversation and re-posing questions from the caucus group activity. Each caucus group will have 10 minutes to discuss the posted questions and at the conclusion of the final inner group's discussion they will debrief the activity.

Large Group Debrief (20 minutes):
Rearrange the room so that the seating is in one large circle and that all students are able to see one another. Engage students in a discussion debriefing both the caucus and fishbowl

activities. Also have student make connections between their experiences, the film, and issues of institutional, cultural, and individual oppression. Suggested questions to pose to the large group are below:

- How did it feel to participate in fishbowl activities?
- Compare your experiences in the inner circle with that of being in the outer circle. Was participating in one circle more comfortable than the other?
- When in the outer circle, what new insights did you learn from the inner group that you did not previous know?
- Based on this activity, what are some themes or patterns you can identify about the ways in which racial oppression manifest in society?
- Reflecting on this activity, what are some next steps we can take to address race-based oppression?

Interdisciplinary Connections:
Social Studies: Have students research news articles that cover the subprime mortgage crisis and financial institution bailout initiative from the U.S. federal government. Have students prepare a brief essay or talking points to discuss patterns or themes they recognized that relate to the Fair Housing Act of 1968.

Supplemental Resources (Optional):
Hardiman, R. and Jackson, B. (2007). Conceptual foundations for social justice education. In M. Adams, L.A. Bell, and P. Griffin (Eds.), *Teaching for diversity and social justice, second edition* (pp. 35-66). New York: Routledge.

Kirp, D. L. (1997). *Our town: Race, housing, and the soul of suburbia.* New Brunswick, New Jersey: Rutgers University Press.

Oppression: Levels & Types Worksheet

Example	Level? Individual | Cultural | Institution	Unconscious/Conscious?	Who is impacted by this example of oppression?

*Adapted in part from "Levels and Types of Oppression" in <u>Teaching for Diversity and Social Justice, Second Edition (2007)</u>.

"What white privilege has afforded us to do is blindly leave our white community and go to a big city and displace African Americans and displace immigrants and displace the children of immigrants and the grandchildren of immigrants and displace the great- grandchildren of immigrants and not think that we are responsible because we think that we are victims, too."

-Danny Hoch, 'Till The White Day is Done interview

"When We Discover Ourselves, We'll be Free": Developing Pathways toward Racial Liberation

Author: Andrea Dre Domingue

Grades: 8-12+

Suggested Time Allowance: 90 minutes

Subject Areas: Life Skills

Materials:
Copies of the *Pathways Toward Liberation Worksheet*
Pens
Markers
Chart Paper

Overview: In this lesson students will explore the concept of liberation in the context of race and begin to strategize ways in which they can individually develop a liberatory consciousness to address racial injustice.

Vocabulary: liberation, ally, consciousness

Objectives:
- Students will be able to imagine and describe their personal visions of liberation.
- Students will be able to identify several tangible ways to work toward racial liberation based on the four elements of developing a liberatory consciousness.

Evaluation/Assessment:
Students will be evaluated based participation in the large group activities and their writings articulating their vision and steps toward liberation.

Activities/Procedures:
1. Step into the Circle (15 minutes):
   Have students stand up and arrange themselves into a circle. Inform students that a series of statements will be read aloud and that if a statement applies to them, they are to step into the circle. Ask students to participate in this activity silently.

   At the conclusion of this activity, lead students in a discussion about any thoughts or emotions that may have surfaced while participating. Encourage students to particularly focus on statements that were difficult to respond to, what it felt like to be one of many or few inside and outside the circle, patterns they observed, etc.

2. Visions of Liberation (45 minutes):

Ask students to take a moment and reflect on the society and world in which they live as it relates to race and race-based oppression. Next ask students to imagine a world where racial injustice does not exists. Distribute paper and markers to students and have them create a drawing that represents their image of racial liberation. Once finished, have students walk around the room with their drawings and share what they created with others, encouraging them to speak to every individual in the room if possible. Once everyone has had a chance to share their visions of liberation, ask students to post their visions around the room and take one final, silent viewing of the group's drawings.

Note to Educators: When scheduling and designing a session on liberation, action, and ally-ship, it is suggested to consider challenges individuals face with following through and sustaining commitment toward social change. It is suggested that educators either find ways of incorporating concepts on liberation early and consistently throughout curriculum schedules and designs.

3. Developing a Liberatory Consciousness (30 minutes):
   Introduce the concept of liberatory consciousness and its four elements: awareness, analysis, action, accountability/ally-ship from the article "Developing a Liberatory Consciousness" in the book Readings for Diversity and Social Justice (full reference listed in the supplemental resources section). Briefly summarized:
   - Liberatory consciousness: a mindfulness of systems of oppression and how individuals have been and are continually socialized to play roles in maintaining these systems. In addition to this recognition a liberatory consciousness empowers individuals to take actions to interrupt oppressive acts and institutions with the ultimate goal of deconstructing these systems.
   - Liberatory consciousness has for elements:
     o *Awareness*- to take notice of one's behavior and attitudes as well as an attention to events and actions of others in person's surroundings.
     o *Analysis*- applying critical thinking to what is now noticed as well as making decisions on how to interpret and respond to a situation.
     o *Action*- the decision and follow-through of steps that need to be taken to address a given situation on an individual or collective level.
     o *Accountability/Ally-ship*- establishing a support network of individuals that will encourage and sustain one's commitment to recognition, analysis, and action.

After providing this overview, distribute the "Pathways toward Liberation Worksheet" and have students create a personal plan to work toward their liberation vision as conceptualized in the previous activity. Once students have completed this worksheet, have them find a partner and discuss what was written on each person's sheet.

Note to Educators: It might be helpful students to think about how they can take steps toward liberation gradually over time by asking students to think of actions they can take immediately, within a week, within a month, or within a year. It is also important to remind students that liberation can be viewed as an ongoing process that is ever-changing, as well as an outcome to move toward.

Extension Activity:
1. As a homework assignment, ask students to write a personal narrative further reflecting on ways they can move toward liberation by having them consider challenges they may face in taking action, strategies for maintaining accountability/ally-ship, and identifying resources to support their efforts.

2. Have students write a personal agreement for themselves, noting ways in which they plan to work toward liberation over a specific amount of time (e.g. month, end of a semester, etc.). Ask students to place these agreements in envelopes that they will then seal and label. Collect envelopes, and when the specific amount of time has passed, redistribute the envelopes. Have students read the personal agreement they wrote for themselves then lead them in a discussion about the degree to which they followed through or faced challenges in committing to their agreements. Students can also respond to these personal statements as a reflective paper.

Interdisciplinary Connections:
History: Have students read write a response paper on historical examples of how individuals and groups worked toward liberation through social movements.

Supplemental Resources (Optional):

Bell, L. A, Washington, S, Weinstein, G and Love, Barbara, (2007). Knowing ourselves as social justice educators. In M. Adams, L.A. Bell, and P. Griffin (Eds.), *Teaching for diversity and social justice, second edition* (pp. 381-393). New York: Routledge.

Harro, B. (2000). Cycle of liberation. In M. Adams, et al. (Eds.), *Readings for diversity and social justice* (pp.463-469). New York: Routledge.

hooks, b. (1994). *Teaching to transgress: Education as the practice of freedom.* New York: Routledge.

Love, B.J. (2000). Developing a liberatory consciousness. In M. Adams, et al. (Eds.), *Readings for diversity and social justice* (pp.470-474). New York: Routledge.

Step Into The Circle: Exploring Liberation

1. I am passionate about working with others.

2. I am passionate about issues of social justice and equity.

3. I have been hurt by racial injustice, inequality, and/or oppression.

4. I have believed a stereotype about my race or ethnic identity.

5. I have believed a stereotype about a race or ethnic identity different than my own.

6. I have been afraid to challenge someone on a racist act or belief because of how I thought it would impact our relationship.

7. I have been punished or ignored when naming a racial injustice or speaking up about something that did not seem fair to me.

8. I have observed racial oppression or injustice being enacted and I did not know what to do or how to react.

9. There has been a time in my life where I found it difficult to share my experience or voice my opinion because I thought I might be labeled a racist person.

10. I have felt guilty for not doing enough to challenge race-based discrimination or injustice.

11. I am beginning to feel more comfortable challenging racial injustice.

12. I believe that ending race-based oppression is possible and feasible.

*Adapted from Domingue, A. D.; Hughbanks, C. (2009, October 2). NEACUHO train the trainer diversity session: Internalized oppression. University of Massachusetts at Amherst, Amherst, MA.

Pathways Toward Liberation Worksheet

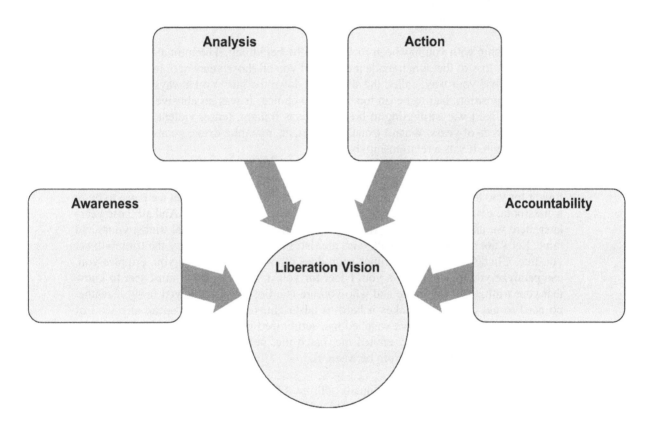

Developed by Andrea Dre Domingue and adapted from "Developing a Liberatory Consciousness" by Barbara J. Love in <u>Readings for Diversity and Social Justice.</u>

A Love Letter from Esther Armah:
Dear John, The Power of the Lens

A love letter. That's what I've been asked to write. How do I do that? Where do I start? I do not love you. So maybe this should be a 'dear John' letter, a break up letter, where I go back and look at our dysfunctional, inter-dependent, inter-connected relationship, minus hatred or rose colored lenses. Except that our history keeps us connected, and leave though I try, I keep running into you everywhere I go; damn. Okay, forget about the dear John part. Let's just share. Me first.

My relationship with you has been rocky from the beginning. The intimate tongue of the lash, and the kiss of the lynch made me wary of you all those years ago. In the beginning you always had your way, called the shots, laid down the law. You always demanded the missionary position, had to be on top. I had no choice. It was an abusive relationship. I always felt like I was struggling to breathe. It was fraught, tense, violent, scary. It went on for hundreds of years. Wasn't exactly a marriage, no white dress, no aisle, no flowers, no honeymoon. It was a relationship though.

Change came. As it always does. I stopped working for you—at least in that capacity. I fought for you to recognize my humanity, blood was shed so I could get a chance to be in a classroom, graduate, go to college, work for myself—or indeed you. And all these years later, here we are. What we have run from is our truths; our individual truths; yours and mine. Let's not run anymore. Walk with me. Isn't love truth? Some say the truth will set you free. Cliché? Maybe. Sometimes truth does other things. It binds you, cripples you, can paralyze you, even destroys you. I feel for you. I wonder how it must feel to know that your truth, what you have and who you are is a lie, wasn't achieved fairly. Breathe, no need to get defensive. Makes it hard to talk right, really hard to speak any kind of truth. Another truth? You have watched me, scrutinized me, labeled me, categorized me, despised me, yearned for me, envied me, hated me, been scared of me—and then you voted for me. I vote for some truth between us.

Let the past be the past, you continually tell me. Okay. I can do that. First though, you need to hear how it affected us. You were lied to. When you described me as savage, less than, ignorant, unworthy—those were lies you told yourself and were told. Not just that I was less than, I mean that you were somehow better, more human, more noble. That too was your lie, your burden, your privilege, ultimately, your cancer. You carry that to this day. That's why you won't be part of something I'm part of. You insist on taking it over, invading it, razing it to the ground, re-writing it or re-telling it. The hero is always you; you either saved me or killed me. Or pitied me. You were hoodwinked, bamboozled. And now, you're suffering, the world that gave you so much is taking away those things that made you, you; that gave you esteem, a sense of value. That's the danger of the single story. You can't always be the hero; you weren't. You were the villain, the criminal.

So now, it's time to just be. It's hard to swallow the resentment, the call to criticize, chastise, wail on you. I'm trying. Give me a minute. This is tough. Who might I have been with your path? Who might you have been with mine? We never got to walk in each other's shoes for a minute, much less a mile. So, no more single stories. No more versions of you where you rescue or save me. Our weird inter-dependent need has created cowards and built careers. Guilt has been the commodity that paved a lot of paths; truth was much harder to come by. We need each other. Admit it. I know it's hard, but you did. Me too. Our versions of ourselves are connected due to our pasts. Were then. Still are. You need me. Still do. You like Ali, think you're the greatest. It ain't bad, it just ain't true. Your version of me was your truth, your way of getting by. I survived us, our relationship; I got scars; you do too.

Now I watch you, read you, listen to you, and hear myself defined by you all over again. Whether it's the small screen, the big screen, the airwaves, the page—your version of me continues to provoke me, make me mad all over again. Now though, I challenge you. You voted for someone who looks like me, so no longer can a single story of your version of me dominate the lens. You gotta get up when I walk in, gotta call me Massa, or maybe just President. Low blow, couldn't resist that one. Look how far we've come, you say; some of us say that too. And yet. And yet. Recent natural disasters remind me that your single story, your single version of who I am stays with you, in your brain, in your soul, you're fixated. You mean well. You don't mean any harm. That's what you say. But you cause harm. You do.

Your lens on my body has always been intrusive, zooming in, close up, nothing hidden, everything exposed. That lens didn't stop me from navigating around it, over it, underneath it to get to where I stand today. Here we are. You and me. I realize we have a strange inter-dependence. You became my fall guy, my guarantee for blame; I continued to be who you perceived and portrayed me to be, someone you wanted, despised, feared, envied. Why? Why are you so attached to this single story of me? Why must you define me in these boxes and by these terms? Is that what your path did to you; robbed you of an ability to measure me beyond that single story.

Time to challenge you and do for me. So, my truth is this; there are no single stories—not yours, not mine. There is a power in the lens, to shape, re-write, re-tell and re-package various truths. To whittle, mold, sand everything down into the single story. There are perspectives, versions, sides. You want absolutes, I can't give you those. That's what lies do, make things absolute; makes them black and white. Truth is much harder, much grayer, more painful, but much more freeing. So, here we are, you and me. The power of the lens. No more single stories. What now?

Esther Armah is a radio host, playwright, author, and award winning international journalist. She has worked in print, radio, and television in the U.S., UK, and Africa. She now lives in New York.

Being an Ally

Author: Tanesha Barnes

Grades: 8-12+

Suggested Time Allowance: 90 minutes

Subject Areas: Life Skills

Materials:
10 Steps to Becoming an Ally PowerPoint or Handout
Blackboard or Newsprint
Markers

Overview: In this lesson students will explore what it means to be an ally and steps to becoming an ally.

Vocabulary: Ally, Guilt

Objectives:
- To provide students with the opportunity to explore ways that they can serve as an ally
- To introduce students to the levels and types of oppression.
- To reflect on Adeeba Rana's poem "Dear white boy" and story that it tells of her experience with others.

Activities/Procedures:
1. <u>What is an Ally (25 minutes):</u> Ask students to take 5 minutes to quietly write on a sheet of paper what they believe an ally is. Tell students not to write their names on their paper. After all students have completed this task, collect the sheets, shuffle them and pass it out to the group. Inform students that they should not say anything if they receive their own sheet, as none of the other students in the group would be aware. After all of the sheets have been read, inform students that you will now together as a group to come up a group definition of ally.

   Allies are members of the advantaged group who act against the oppression (s) from which they derive power, privilege and acceptance.

   Inform students that within the social manifestation of racism white people are the advantaged group and People of Color: African Americans, Asian Americans, Latinos, Native Americans and Multiracial/Biracial people are the oppressed group.

2. <u>10 Steps to Becoming an Ally (40 minutes)</u>: Ask students for examples of someone being an ally to another person. Take a few examples and then inform students that we will now go through 10 steps to becoming an ally. These are only ten key points in ally development. They are not meant to be a complete list of all of the ways that can be an ally.

<u>10 Steps to Becoming an Ally Handout (Adapted from a presentation by Marcella Runell Hall@copyright2010).</u>

Being an ally is a responsibility *that requires humility and integrity and should not be taken lightly*. It is not about being a savior, nor does it require you to be an expert on someone else's experience. However, it does require that you believe oppression is wrong whether it is happening directly to you or not, and that you are prepared to deal with the consequences of speaking up and/or acting against injustice.

Step One: Definitions (Know what you are talking about)
Diversity is a complex interplay of multiple social identities and issues including gender, race, ethnicity, socioeconomic class, religion or spiritual affiliation, sexual orientation, national origin, age, physical, emotional & developmental ability and language.

Adams, Bell and Griffin (1997) define social justice as both a process and a goal. "The goal of social justice is full and equal participation of all groups in a society that is mutually shaped to meet their needs. Social justice includes a vision of society that is equitable and all members are physically and psychologically safe and secure."

Diversity is who we are; social justice is what we do.

Step Two: Privilege
Learn what it means to have privilege based on your social identities and social location.

Step Three: Social Power
Continue or begin to explore how social power works in U.S. society and globally- who has it and who doesn't, and why.

Step Four: Oppression
Gain awareness of the levels and types of oppression: Individual, Cultural and Institutional (see chart).

	Individual	Cultural	Institutional
Unconscious	I don't see you as... (colorblind ideology)	-Women as "bad" drivers -Standards of beauty	-Subprime loans -Patriot Act -No Child Left Behind
Conscious	-Racist/sexist/ heterosexist jokes -Superiority Ideology	-TV & Films Tokenism -Stereotyping Positive or Negative	-Marriage Laws -Red-Lining -Jim Crow -Patriot Act

Step Five: Awareness
Learn your own history. (*A People's History of the United States* by Howard Zinn is a good place to start).

Step Six: (White) Guilt
Work through any guilt you might about having privilege. While guilt is a natural response to learning about unearned privilege, it is quite damaging because it centers the story/process/group back on the privileged person - which is typically the opposite of what would be liberating for the group. Working through guilt and finding a proactive positive outlet is not only beneficial, but a necessity in becoming an ally.

Step Seven: Finding Support
Find a group of friends, colleagues, and/or classmates who will keep you honest about your work as an ally and make sure they have agreed to be your accountability person or people.

Step Eight: Research
DO YOUR OWN RESEARCH- do not expect other people to take the responsibility for educating you about their experience. Take classes, check out web sites, attend a lecture, step out of your comfort zone and take the learning into your own hands.

Step Nine: Making Mistakes
Don't be afraid to make mistakes. Hone your instincts and be sincere in your efforts. Operating with integrity will take you much further than being fearful.

Step Ten: Listen
Listen to other people's experiences- if people are willing to share with you listen with an open heart and an open mind-it is a gift to be treasured, even when it is hard to hear.

3. Dear White Boy (30 minutes): Read the poem, "Dear white boy" by Adeeba Rana to the group.

Dear white boy by Adeeba Rana

One,

I have no elephant god.

No swami-like turban. No Golden Temple.

Two,

Recently, you apologized for an insulting comment,

to the wrong friend.

Their "ghetto" styles must have thrown you off, but no matter,

all Filipinas look alike anyways.

Three,

As my eyes brewed quick, muddy anger,

you seemed startled at my rage,

hurt that I couldn't handle "a little joke"

offended that I didn't take the time to educate you.

Four,

Guess what white boy, that is not my job.

I am not your bridge,

I am not your teacher,

and I sure as hell am not your filter.

Five,

I thought I was your friend,

but as you so genuinely told me the other day,

the only difference between Pakistan, Bangladesh and India were those three little

lines of demarcation on the globe.

You turned 75 years of struggle; children eating the dust of refugee roads,

nostrils filled with the stench of burning flesh,

bodies bruised with the rubble that used to be home,

into three lines on a map.

Six,

White boy,

touch that line.

See if your hands do not come away with

the blood of my people.

Hold the war-torn souls of my brothers and sisters in your palms,

look me in the eye and tell me I don't understand.

I will believe you.

With the tears of ghost-like orphans running down my cheeks, the hollowed stomachs

of my hungry, and the gnarled hands of my poor,

I will clutch at you,

and tell you I am the one who doesn't understand

-Adeeba Afshan Rana is a South Asian-American poet, activist, and educator.

Processing Questions:
- What are your initial reactions to the poem "Dear white boy"?
- What is the message that Adeeba Rana is trying to get across with this poem?
- What if any relationship does this poem have with being an ally?

1. <u>Take Aways (5 minutes)</u>: Ask students to close out the day's lesson by sharing a take away with the group. (A takeaway is a new insight or idea that they will take with them).

Extended Activity:
Provide students with the 10 Steps to Being an Effective Ally Worksheet and ask them complete it.

10 Steps to Being an Effective Ally Worksheet

Please select one community or issue that you would like to serve as an ally to.

1. Be clear on your perspective, rules, and expectations.

What perspectives does your background bring? How does this affect the way you reach out as an ally?

[   ]

What are your own rules?

[   ]

What are your expectations?

[   ]

2. Recognize where you have privilege.

In what areas do you see yourself having privilege?

[   ]

How does this affect your role as an ally?

[   ]

3. Explore how social power works within the U.S. societal context.
Who has power and who doesn't, and why?

[ ]

4. Deepen your awareness of the levels and types of oppression.
Please list examples of oppression that the community or issue that you have chosen faces in regards to:

Institutional:

Cultural:

Individual:

How do these aspects interact?

[ ]

5. Know Your Historical Context, and share it.
What is your historical context and story? How can you share it with others?

[ ]

What is the historical context of the community or issue you are serving as an ally for? How can you learn more about it?

[ ]

6. Make the most of your own unique skills, talents and abilities.
What can you contribute?

How can you serve as a role model?

7. Find a group of friends, colleagues, classmates, neighbors, family members who will keep you honest about your role as an ally. You need support and renewed energy to be able to work effectively as an ally.
Who are the people that can keep you 'on track'?

How will you set up a system to make sure that you are receiving and giving the support that you need?

8. Accept that you will make mistakes.
What would you like to improve upon in the future?

9. Take care of yourself.

How can you take responsibility for your own learning?

What courses can you take or events can you attend to learn more?

Where can you find sources of information?

How can you step outside of your comfort zone?

10. Listen.

Who can you listen to? Who do you know that have stories that are willing to share?

How can serve as a better listener?

*Adapted in part from "Action Planning" in <u>Teaching for Diversity and Social Justice, Second Edition (2007).</u>

Supplemental Activity:
Processing Guilt Around Privilege

Author: Samantha Shapses Wertheim

Grades: 8-12+

Suggested Time Allowance: 90 minutes

Subject Areas: Life Skills

Materials:
Journals / paper
Index cards
Pens
Art Supplies

Overview: This lesson will help participants process the guilt that they may experience as they learn more about systems of privilege and oppression in society.

Objectives:
- To create awareness of issues of guilt with group members
- To learn and discuss appropriate ways of processing guilt
- To assist in identifying positive and appropriate support networks

Note to Educators: The following exercises can be done consecutively, or separately.

Actions Procedures
1. Propose the following question: Why do you think we are talking about guilt? After participants answer, explain that guilt is a natural and real part of the process of learning more about privilege. (5 minutes)

2. Pass out the index cards and ask each participant to think of one aspect of their life that they experience privilege. Examples of privilege can be found in race, class, abelism, sexual orientation, gender, education, etc. Then ask the participants to answer two questions anonymously on their index card (20 minutes)
   - Have you ever felt guilty because of the privilege you experience?
   - What do you feel guilty about?
   When the index cards are completed, collect, shuffle them, and pass one out to each participant. Ask the participants to read the index card out loud, instruct them that even if they receive their own, no one will know that it is theirs.

3. Write it down (15 minutes)

It is important that we are processing our guilt in the right setting. We must find ways to process our guilt about privilege that do not involve engaging the target group. One method is journaling.

Write the term Journaling on the board and ask the students if any of them keep a journal. If so ask them what kind of stuff do they journal about? Feelings? Daily Activities? Future Aspirations?

We are going to practice a journal exercise that focuses on processing your guilt.

Think about the last time that you felt guilt over privilege. In your journal write the following:
- Explain what happened to trigger the guilt.
- How did you feel?
- How did you deal with the guilt?

When the students have finished writing in their journal, ask them how it felt to write it down and get the feelings out of their head and onto paper.

4. Get Creative – Abstract Art (25 minutes)

One method of processing any feeling is to be creative. Write the term Abstract Art on the board. Ask the students if they know what abstract art is. After they have contributed, explain that with abstract art there are no rules, it is simply an expression of what they are feeling. Abstract art does not have to 'look' like anything, it is a collection of shapes and forms that come together to create a picture.

Now we will be creating an abstract art piece based on our feelings of guilt.

Ask the students to close their eyes and ask them the following questions: (20 minutes)

What color is guilt?
What shape is it? Is it jagged? Is it soft?
What is the pattern of your guilt? Is it busy? Is it calm?
What is the size of your guilt? It is a large picture, is it detailed?

Using the vision in your head, please take the art supplies and begin to draw about the quote you chose. Contemplate using your journal entry to inspire you. You can include images, words, and colors – anything that you feel expresses yourself.

Afterwards, the drawings can be hung up to create a gallery space that the students can view.

5. Finding friends (10 minutes)

Is there anyone that you can speak to that may share the same feelings of guilt as you? Processing guilt with the appropriate people is an important aspect of overcoming guilt. Let's explore the following

- Make a list of appropriate people that you can talk to.
- Search for the relevant organizations that have meetings or programs which discuss privilege.
- Look for online resources or social networking sites that connect people. who are experiencing the same feelings about privilege and oppression.
- Join organizations or support groups that focus on being an ally to target groups.

6. Accept and Move-On (10 minutes)

Experiencing guilt means that you are also experiencing awareness! Accept the fact that guilt is a natural part of the process for many people and focus on what you can do to assist in serving as an ally. And look for creative outlets or other healthy and productive ways to unlearn oppressive behaviors that hinder your work as an ally.

A Love Letter from Tim Wise

Dear White America,

Forgive me for writing you one big letter, rather than taking the time to compose some 200 million separate ones, personalize 'em and seal 'em with a great big kiss. But I got some shit to do, and not a lot of time in which to do it, so for now, just consider this a group hug.

Yeah, I know, a hug is not what you were expecting. Not from me anyway. I mean, I'm one of you—a member of the club, so to speak—but still, sometimes I get the impression that you think I don't much like you. In fact, just the other day, one of our 200 million wrote me to ask why it was I hate white people so much.

Same stuff I hear on a regular: Tim Wise hates white people. Tim Wise hates himself. Crazy stuff. And I just wanted to make sure we were straight, you and me, 'cuz, ya' know, I don't want to be misunderstood. Besides, fact is, not only do I *not* hate you—I mean, us—I actually love you, blemishes and all: hell, oozing sores and all, I still love you. I don't always feel so hot about what you—I mean, we—have done. Nor am I real big on loving the unearned privileges and advantages we get just for lack of melanin. But hating *that* is not the same as hating white people. That stuff is about whiteness, which isn't the same as you, in case you didn't know that. Whiteness and white supremacy are systemic things, but you're just folks, caught up in the bullshit like everyone else. The only difference is, some of y'all don't know it yet.

Really it's sorta funny, ya know? To be accused of hating white people just because you speak out against white privilege and white racism. I mean, think it through with me: if being against white racism makes a person "anti-white" then doesn't that mean that racism is like the *essence* of being white? Doesn't it mean that being *pro* white racism is somehow the only way to show your love for white people? Doesn't it mean that white people and racism are pretty much synonymous? Or at least like an old married couple? Messed up, dontcha' think? I mean, seriously, have you ever considered that? How ass-backwards it is to basically decide that we are collectively so evil, you and me, that we just can't help ourselves, and that trying to break free from the conditioning we've been exposed to is somehow to betray one another? It's sorta' like saying that for a man to critique rape is to be anti-male, which is to say that rape is the essence of masculinity. Now *that* is self-hating.

You see, and I may be wrong in this, but I think you're better than that—that we are. I'm convinced we have choices. I know we do, because I've seen people exercise them, and even made some myself. I know that for every Andrew Jackson—land stealing, Indian killing bastard that he was—there's a Jeremiah Evarts standing up against him and saying no. For every John Calhoun, defending the system of enslavement, there's a John Fee, challenging it, refusing to even provide communion to parishioners in his church so long as they owned other human beings, and willing to be defrocked for his insolence. For every Bull Connor there's a Virginia Durr; for every George Wallace a Bob or Dottie Zellner. And yes, I know that for most of you, these names I mention in praise, and in contrast to the others, won't even be recognizable. And I also know that there's a reason for that; and it's one you ought to ask yourself about from time to time.

Ask yourself why you know so well the names of those whose lives were defined by the cruelty they meted out to others, why you know the names and maybe even the biographies of the worst amongst us, but almost nothing about the best, almost nothing about those in our little tribe who placed their humanity—ours—above the conceit of skin alone. And trust me when I tell you, once you allow yourself to really think about why you know the one but not the other, the answers that will come to you won't be the comforting kind. They'll be answers you might wish you'd never known. The kind that make you realize that somewhere, along the way, whiteness tricked you too. In this case, it made you identify with the perpetration of injustice, and to jealously defend your own reputation from critique, even as you had these other role models all along, right there waiting for you to join them, to follow in their footsteps. And had you joined them, your reputation wouldn't be half as sullied as it is now by virtue of your silence, your defensiveness, your denial.

So are you ready then? Are we? Ready to choose again, and this time, perhaps get it right? Ready to choose again, and this time, to live in this skin differently? Ready to relinquish the bonds that we have placed around our own bodies and minds, thanks to white supremacy? Ready to join the circle of humanity, but this time merely as equals, rather than as lords and masters?

I mean, it's your choice, and I'll keep loving you no matter what you decide. We're too tightly bound for me to do otherwise. But really now, the clock is ticking, time is tight, and all the world is dying, quite literally, for your answer. So think it over, but get back at me quickly. We have some shit to do. And not a lot of time in which to do it.

With Love,

Tim Wise

Tim Wise is among the nation's most prominent white antiracist educators, writer and activists. He is the author of five books on race and racism, and lectures across the United States about institutional racism, white privilege and the ongoing struggle for justice and equity.

PART TWO

Appropriate or Appreciate?
A Reflection on Cultural Appropriation

Author: Samantha Shapses Wertheim

Grades: 8-12+

Suggested Time Allowance: 90 minutes

Subject Areas: Language, Sociology, Marketing, Communications, Media

Materials:
Large post-it pad or blackboard
White board markers
Markers
Examples of cultural appropriation and cultural appreciation, and set up (media player, computer, DVD, power point if necessary)
Quotes for reflection
Liberation grid

Overview: In this lesson students will create a collective definition of cultural appropriation and engage in an activity that creates discussion around cultural appropriation and cultural appreciation.

Vocabulary: Culture, Appropriation, Agent, Target

Objectives:
- To collectively define cultural appropriation, with a working knowledge of what it means and how it is used.
- To discuss the difference between cultural appropriation and cultural appreciation.
- To reflect upon aspects of cultural appropriation in the hip hop community.

Activities/Procedures:
Part I (50 minutes total)

1. To begin the lesson write Cultural Appropriation and Cultural Appreciation on separate sides of the board:

2. Pass out the definition sheet below, and ask for one volunteer per definition to read the word out loud. (5 minutes)

Definitions	
Culture	The customary beliefs, social forms, and material traits of a racial, religious, or social group; the characteristic features of everyday existence shared by people in a place or time ("Merriam-Webster Dictionary")
Appropriation	To take or make use of without authority or right ("Merriam-Webster Dictionary")
Appreciation	An expression of admiration, approval, or gratitude ("Merriam-Webster Dictionary")
Cultural	Of or relating to a culture ("Merriam-Webster Dictionary")
Agent	The members of a social identity group which have greater access to social power and privilege based upon membership in their social group (Hardiman, Jackson and Griffin, 2007)
Target	The members of a social identity group whose access to power is limited or denied (Hardiman, Jackson and Griffin, 2007)

3. After the students have finished reading the words divide the students up into groups of two or three depending on class size.

   Instruct the students that using the definitions they should create a definition for Cultural Appropriation and Cultural Appreciation that they will share with the group. (15 minutes)

4. When the students have finished, ask each group to read their definition of cultural appropriation and cultural appreciation. While they are reading write some of the terms and ideas from their definitions on the board under the term. If something is repeated you can place a check mark next to that word for emphasis. (20 – 30 minutes depending on class size)

5. When all of the terms and ideas have been listed ask
   a) Can someone summarize these two definitions?
   b) What is the difference between cultural appropriation and cultural appreciation?
   c) Can anyone give an example of cultural appropriation vs. cultural appreciation?

   If necessary, review the definition

   Cultural appropriation is the adoption or appropriation of some specific elements of one by a different cultural group. It denotes acculturation or assimilation, but often connotes a negative view towards acculturation from a minority culture by a dominant culture. It can include the introduction of forms of dress or personal adornment, music and art, religion, language, or social behavior. These elements, once removed from their indigenous cultural contexts, may take on meanings that are significantly divergent from, or merely less nuanced than, those they originally held. Or, they may be stripped of meaning altogether. ("Art and popular," 2008)

Part II (65 minutes total): The next section will be an activity to further define and spark conversation about cultural appropriation and cultural appreciation.

1. On the right side of the room hang a sign that says APPROPRIATE, on the left side of the room hang a sign that says APPRECIATE
2. Explain to the students that you will show them a picture, state a fact or play a video. If they think that something is being appropriated, they should move over to right side, if they think something is being appreciated, they should move to the left side. If they are unsure, or think that it is a combination, they should move some place in the middle of the signs.
3. Appropriate/Appreciate Activity (20 minutes)
   Choose 10 examples of cultural appropriation or appreciation to show to the students. Examples can include magazines, books, pictures, clips of films, music videos or TV shows. Here are some examples:

   The following examples can be found at www.jlovecalderon.com

   - A picture or clip of Elvis Presley
   - A picture or clip of Eminem
   - A foreign film with English subtitles
   - A picture of Paris Hilton, and a 'That's Hot' T-shirt
   - A picture of a Chinese character tattoo
   - A picture of a lotus flower tattoo
   - A picture of Henna non-related to an Indian ceremony
   - An African dance class
   - A hip hop concert
   - A book about Yoga
   - An advertisement for Yoga clothing
   - Slang now used in popular media or advertisements

   After some of the examples ask the students why they chose appropriate, appreciate or somewhere in the middle. Ask the students on different sides so that both can share their opinions.

4. Process the activity by asking the students the following questions: (10 minutes)
   - What did you think about that exercise?
   - Were there any examples that surprised you? What were they?
   - Can you think of more examples of cultural appropriation or cultural appreciation?
   - What are you taking away from this exercise?

Extension Activities:

1. Reflect (15 minutes or take home):
   Using the following 3 quotes from 'Til the White Day is Done allow the students 10 minutes to reflect on cultural appropriation and hip-hop culture.

   What do you think about the quotes below? Do you agree or disagree with M1, MC Serch, and Talib Kweli?

   "You don't have to say Hip Hop and racism, you can say African culture and racism because Hip Hop was exploited and robbed by the same culprits who have robbed us down the line since the discovery of the drums, since the discovery of the wisdom in ancient Egypt.... So I think when you talk about the theft of a culture, you talk about Hip Hop and Jazz, our art as a whole." – M1, 'Til the White Day is Done

   "I think it is unfair to say that Eminem is Elvis. Elvis stole from black people, Eminem didn't steal from black people. His whole crew was black, the only people he kept around him were black people. Everyone that benefited from his growth were black." – MC Serch, 'Til the White Day is Done

   "If you have respect for people and know right from wrong, you don't have to describe yourself as anti-racist. People just see it. And…as far as the music… just to have real respect for the culture….and education is important. I know what it takes for a white person to be accepted in the Black community or to be accepted as 'down' with a black art form. The ingredients center around respect, and being educated about the culture." – Talib Kweli, 'Til the White Day is Done

2. Liberate (15 minutes or take home):
   Ask the students to complete the exercise as a take home or in class.
   Is there an activity, hobby, or passion that you have that stems from another culture? How can you learn more about it its origin and culture?

Activity / Hobby / Passion	
Books I can read:	
Websites I can visit:	
People I can talk to:	
Classes I can take:	
Additional explorations:	

Interdisciplinary Connections:

Geography: Using a map of the world visually mark the origins of items that have been appropriated. Ask the students for suggestions of appropriated items, or provide a list yourself. For example: yoga practiced in India, hip-hop's roots in Africa, Chinese figure tattoos to calligraphy in China, etc.

Supplemental Resources (Optional):

White Like Me; Code of Ethics for White Kid in Hip-Hop by JLove

www.daveyd.com/commentary**white**likeme.html

Works Cited

Appreciation. (2010). In *Merriam-Webster Online Dictionary*. Retrieved January 24, 2010, from http://www.merriam-webster.com/dictionary/appreciation.

Appropriation. (2010). In *Merriam-Webster Online Dictionary*. Retrieved January 24, 2010, from http://www.merriam- webster.com/dictionary/appropriation.

Art and popular culture. (2008, February 8). Retrieved from http://www.artandpopularculture.com/Cultural_appropriation.

Culture. (2010). In *Merriam-Webster Online Dictionary*. Retrieved January 24, 2010, from http://www.merriam-webster.com/dictionary/culture

Cultural. (2010). In *Merriam-Webster Online Dictionary*. Retrieved January 24, 2010, from http://www.merriam-webster.com/dictionary/cultural

Hardiman, R., Jackson, B. & Griffin, P.(2007) Conceptual Foundations for Social Justice Education. In M. Adams, L.A. Bell, & P. Griffin (Eds.), Teaching for Diversity and Social Justice (pp. 35-66). New York, NY: Taylor & Francis Group, LLC

A Love Letter from Peggy McIntosh

January 25, 2010

I am writing this love letter to all those teachers who have been teaching about privilege systems, including white privilege, during the last 20 years. It has been a hard row to hoe, and the far right has tried its best to squelch the conversation and intimidate teachers who undertake it.

If you have been teaching about privilege I want to salute your bravery and your intellectual integrity. Most of us were not taught about privilege, in so many words, if at all. Those of us who had overadvantage of any kind probably were not introduced to that as an important concept, and so we could not use the concept as an intellectual tool. I imagine that the reason why you are using it now, if you are white, or born to financial security, or male, or heterosexual, or Anglo-European, is that it has explained things for you that were kept opaque during your childhood. My guess is that you feel that the concept of overadvantage has made your perceiving and understanding more accurate.

The schools and universities in which you teach think of themselves as passing on accurate and important knowledge. These are some of the 'givens' of education. But you have gone further, trying to correct inaccuracy and partial vision. You have chosen to do something very hard. You have been helping students in this individualistically-based knowledge culture to see systemically. If you have been teaching in such a way that you help students to see power differentials in society, you have been doing what is still pretty unspeakable in American culture—addressing power, putting it beside the claims of the United States to liberty and justice for all, and critiquing the actual conditions of life in the United States, as well as your past education.

You have made a huge difference. It may not look this way from where you sit in your institutions. I am speaking from my perspective as someone who travels to many non-academic locations. I find that outside the academic world, even those who think they are very aware of race and of power are likely never to have heard of white privilege or any other kind of privilege. They will not have heard about it from the newspapers, TV, magazines, ministers, lawyers, doctors, merchants, pundits, opinion-makers, filmmakers, artists, dramatists or musicians.

But when I travel to schools, colleges, and universities I meet students and colleagues for whom privilege is a living subject and one which they are willing to face, regardless of the risks to ego, identity, security, safety, and social location. I am very grateful to teachers who have taken the risk of ending the kinds of silences that they were schooled with themselves.

Last summer in Washington, D.C., I attended a conference called Race and Reconciliation which was held at the National Press Club. It was organized by Janet Langhart and her husband, Senator William Cohen. Janet has been a well-known TV commentator and host in the Boston area. Bill was Secretary of Defense during some of Clinton's years in office. They invited some 60 participants from all over the United States, to join in a conversation about race and reconciliation. About 50 presentations for an audience of press and participants identified racial problems and suggested solutions for the 21st Century.

I was dismayed and disappointed by how much was missing from the presentations. The only mention of white privilege as an aspect of racism, perhaps the determining aspect of racism, came from participants who had had exposure to it in schools, colleges or universities. It was striking to me that only this handful of people located vocationally in academic life took for granted the importance of acknowledging white and class privilege when looking at race. They showed two important capacities: first, to think institutionally, rather than simply in terms of individuals; and second, to realize that oppression has an upside -- exemption from oppression -- which is not seen or acknowledged as the force that keeps racism in place.

I left the conference feeling that only the universities and schools are doing the necessary work to raise awareness about privilege systems and to teach the ability to question the United States myth of meritocracy. I felt a new level of respect for people who have worked for the last 20 years in universities making it possible for students to recognize and analyze systemic inequities in U.S. culture. The punishment meted out to teachers and professors who teach their students to see systemically can be severe. It can come from students, parents, colleagues, administrators, alumni, journalists, and pundits of all kinds. Accusations of socialism, denials of tenure or promotion, negative evaluations, and retaliation against faculty by right wing or white supremacists groups can make life very hard for teachers who are making the curriculum more inclusive—lessening white, male, class, U.S., or any other kind of systemic privilege which makes knowledge incomplete and inaccurate, and keeps knowledge systems in the hands of the most powerful.

I feel that seeing white privilege is the missing link between discussing racism and discussing how to end it. So I send this love letter to those who are filling in the missing link and refusing to pretend that we can end oppression while ignoring the oppressiveness that comes with unearned advantage. I honor your sense of integrity. I wish you good colleagueship, strong support from students and other allies, and the courage of your convictions.

Peggy McIntosh, Ph.D., is founder and co-director of the National SEED Project on Inclusive Curriculum (Seeking Educational Equity and Diversity). She is also Associate Director of the Wellesley Centers for Women at Wellesley College. Her most recent articles are: 'White Privilege: An Account to Spend,' and 'White People Facing Race: Uncovering Myths that Keep Racism in Place,' both published in 2009 by the Saint Paul Foundation in St. Paul, MN; and 'Foreword' in Karen Weekes's edited volume 'Privilege and Prejudice: Twenty Years with the Invisible Knapsack,' published in 2009 by Cambridge Scholars Press, UK.

Student Power:
Bridging The Achievement Gap

Author: Piper Anderson

Grades: 8-12 +

Suggested Time Allowance: 90 minutes

Subject Areas: Language Arts

Materials:
Newsprint
Markers
Pens
Paper

Overview: In this lesson students will learn about the achievement gap in education, its causes and consequences for students and communities.

Vocabulary: Achievement, Opportunity

Objective:
- Students will understand the role of race in the educational achievement gap.
- Students will reflect on their own experiences in school and their connection to the achievement gap.
- Students will write about their experiences with education in schools.
- Students use their experience as students to make a 'list of demands' for a better education system.

Activities/Procedures:
1. Web of Connections (15 minutes):
    Before students enter the class write on a piece of newsprint or an eraser board 'Achievement Gap' and draw a circle around the phrase. When students arrive explain that together you will be exploring the achievement gap in education and how it impacts students and communities.

    Pose the following question to students: What words, concepts, ideas, etc. come to mind when you see this term? Chart their responses forming a web around the term. Spend about ten minutes challenging them to identify connections reminding them that there are no right or wrong answers share what ever comes to mind.

    Next provide them with a definition of the Achievement Gap in Education:

The Achievement Gap is the huge difference in academic performance between students from different economic circumstances and racial/ethnic backgrounds.

This definition is taken from the Education Equality Project. Feel free to formulate your own definition. Before moving on to the next exercise check in with students to see that they have any questions about definition.

Question for consideration: Is it more accurate to call this phenomenon an Achievement Gap or an Opportunity Gap?

2. Small Group Discussion (25 minutes):
Divide students into small groups of 3-5 depending on the size of the group and provide each group with a piece of newsprint.

Explain that they will have 10-minutes to discuss the following question: What are the causes of the education achievement gap? Have each group assign a note taker to chart the group's responses.

Once they have generated a list they should identify what they feel is the number one cause of the achievement gap and prepare a creative presentation of their findings for the larger group. The creative presentation could look like a poem/song, scene or skit, or a visual art presentation. Provide each group with an additional 10-15-minutes to prepare their creative presentations.

3. Group Sharing (10-15 minutes):
Each group will share their creative presentations. After the presentations the Facilitator should lists the top three reasons for achievement gap in education, which according to the Education Equality Project are:
> -Teacher Training and Experience
> -School Funding
> -Parental Involvement

4. Partner Reflection (10 minutes):
Students will find a partner and reflect on the following questions:
- What was my best school experience?
- What was my worst school experience?

As each student speaks their partner should be listening for the key ideas that seem jump out in their partner's story. Specifically, did you notice any connections to the achievement gap as discussed in the previous exercise? After their partner has shared they will reflect back those key ideas as a way to deepen the reflection for both of them.

5. My Education Writing Exercise (10 minutes):

Next with a pen and paper students will each write about the experiences they shared with their partner.

Encourage them to be as specific as possible in writing their story and also consider the question *how have my experiences of school impacted the way I feel about education?*

Ask for volunteers to share their writings. For some students this writing may feel very personal so they may not want to share so offer students the opportunity to pass on sharing if they prefer.

6. Student List of Demands: (10 minutes):
To set-up this exercise explain to the group that they deserve and should demand changes in their education. What are your list of demands for a better education?

Hang a large sheet of newsprint on the wall and provide students with markers. Allow them to write their demands for a better education. Remind them to think about the achievement gap and what can be done to close the achievement gap and improve the education of all students.

7. Closing Exercise (5 minutes):
To close the work have the group stand in a circle and ask them to say a word or phrase in response to the question- what's possible if we close the achievement gap? This exercise can be done popcorn style with students throwing words into the circle as they feel moved. Once everyone has contributed and the circle has gone silent the session is complete.

Extension Activity:
1. Writing exercise: "Day in the life of a student..." what challenges to students face toward achieving an education?

Interdisciplinary Connections:
Social Sciences: Create a survey with the question: What can your school district do to close the achievement gap in education? Collect responses from students, parents, and teachers.

Supplemental Reading:

Still Separate, Still Unequal: America's Educational Apartheid by Jonathan Kozol
Harper's Magazine v.311 n. 1864 91/2005

Governor Pataki says an eighth grade education is enough
http://www.greenspun.com/bboard/q-and-a-fetch-msg.tcl?msg_id=009Vxb

Edweek: Achievement Gap
http://www.edweek.org/rc/issues/achievement-gap/

Education Equality Project
http://www.edequality.com

The Achievement Gap Initiative at Harvard University
http://www.agi.harvard.edu

"History and herstory has not been taught properly in this country. They don't teach it at all. And it's on purpose because if they were to teach history and herstory properly in this country then there wouldn't be a question, is there racism in America? There wouldn't be a question, is affirmative action necessary? None of that would be necessary, because the point is you will understand that you had a people who were enslaved; who were not allowed to read or write; not allowed to go to school, and so on…"

-Sonia Sanchez, interviewed by April Silver for 'Til the White Day is Done

A Love Letter from Hectór Calderón

"Freedom is not an ideal located outside of man; nor is it an idea which becomes myth. It is rather the indispensable condition for the quest for human completion."
-Paulo Freire

Dear Educators-

I once heard the poet Saul Williams say that, "Love is the Soul's Imagination." This definition of love has always moved me because he defined it this way: Love requires an act of creativity, an act of invention from a deep place at the center of our being. It is from this place that I write this Love letter to you. As an educator you have taken on the noblest cause in the world: the liberation of the human race. Liberation defined as the process of becoming fully human.

As an educator for many years, I have come to know, as I am sure you know, that schools are not just schools. Schools are a flash of the human spirit. It is the vehicle by which the soul of every teacher and every student comes in to the material world. Schools are not just schools. Schools are an old growth forest of the mind, a watershed of thought. Schools are not just schools. Schools are an ecosystem of the academic and spiritual possibilities.

But we also know that schools are places that can perpetuate lies, that can affirm myths, and oppress the human spirit. When I think about race and racism as the power of an illusion that has been perpetuated in sacred spaces such as the classroom, I think about my own experience as a young person. When I first entered a school in the United States, the first thing I was told was that "I needed to learn English and lose my Spanish." You see inherent in that statement was the understanding that in order to be accepted I needed to become more "American." But as a kid, I always wondered who was the ideal American that I should modeled myself to. The answer became very evident by the people I read about in books, the people I saw as teachers, the people I saw in television, and the leaders I saw in power. They were all white. I remember being very conflicted because nowhere in books or in public spaces did I read about people who looked like me or see people like me. I thought that in order to be accepted I needed to lose everything that made me who I was up to that point. Cultural assimilation became tantamount to cultural annihilation. In my formative years I experienced education as the tool for indoctrination rather than "the practice of freedom, the means by which men and women deal critically and creatively with reality and discover how to participate in the transformation of their world," as the Brazilian educator Paulo Freire would put it.

Dear educators I offer a slice of my experience as a students to remind you of a teachers' first dream: to make a difference in the world. I still believe that true, Liberatory education offers us the best chance to change the world within a generation. Classrooms are these sacred places where each generation must discover their full humanity. While it is true that we must teach invaluable language skills, we must also teach them to use their skills to develop a language of understanding that bridges all cultures. While it is true that we must teach them critical research strategies, we must also teach them to use their insights to serve their communities. While we must cultivate a scientific mind in our students, I would also teach them to use their knowledge to cure diseases of the body and spirit. While we must immerse students in mathematical ideas, we must also help students create equations that lead to equality for all people. While we must teach them artistic skills, we must, more importantly, teach to use their imagination to create the "Imagined Nation."

Hectór Calderón,
Principal, El Puente Academy for Peace and Justice.

A dedicated educator and activist, Héctor Calderón was one of the developing members of the El Puente Academy for Peace & Justice in 1993. El Puente Academy is the first human rights high school in the United States.

What's Wrong With Healthcare?

Author: Piper Anderson

Grades: 8-12+

Suggested Time Allowances: 90 minutes

Subject Area: Social Sciences, Fine Art

Materials:
Pens
Paper
Newsprint
Markers
Poster board

Overview: Students will explore their own relationship to healthcare access. Students will create posters representing a solution to disparities in healthcare.

Objectives:
- Students will understand the racial disparities that exist in healthcare system and how it impacts different communities.

Activities/Procedures:
1. Healthcare Graffiti Board: (15 minutes):
   Before students arrive hang a large piece of newsprint at the top write: What's wrong with healthcare?

   When students arrive offer them markers and allow them to chart their own responses to these question. After everyone has finished writing their responses have the group stand back and read what has been written. Ask them to point out in common themes and ideas that maybe appear multiple times or were reflected in different statements.

2. Healthcare Walk: (25 minutes):
   Explain that all of their responses are valid and today we are going to specifically talk about racial disparities in healthcare.

   Across the room…
   1. If you or your family has lived without health coverage.
   2. If you have health insurance.
   3. If you have a history of diabetes or hypertension in your family.

4. If you have a primary care physician (a personal doctor) who you see at least once per year.
5. If you or someone in your family has been hospitalized.
6. If you travel outside of your neighborhood or community to see a doctor.
7. If you or someone you know has given birth to a child.
8. If you or a family member have paid out of pocket for prescriptions regularly.
9. If you know someone who needs to see a doctor but cannot afford it.
10. If you or someone you know has ever felt like you did not receive the proper care from a physician because of your race or where you lived.

Ask for volunteers to step up and contribute other statements on the theme of inequalities in healthcare. What did you notice participating in this exercise? What questions did it raise for you about access to healthcare?

3. Protest for Better Health: (30 minutes):
Explain that you are now going to create posters with your demands for healthcare. Their poster should address the question: What needs to be done to address the inequalities in healthcare?

Divide students into small groups and provide them with a piece of poster board and markers. Encourage them to draft out what they want their poster to look like on scratch paper before working on their poster.

4. Sharing: (20 minutes):
Allow each group to share their poster sharing their process and the ideas represented in their poster.

Extension Activities:
1. Write letters to your elected official demanding that action be taken to respond to racial disparities in healthcare.
2. Write an op-ed on racial disparities in healthcare and send to your local newspaper.
3. Write a ten-point platform for equity in healthcare.

Interdisciplinary Connection:
Health: Survey students in your school about their access to healthcare and write a report about how disparities in healthcare impact teens.

Resources:
- NY Times: Research Finds Wide Disparities in Healthcare by Race and Region
  http://www.nytimes.com/2008/06/05/health/research/05disparities.html
- National Healthcare Disparities Report 2006
  http://www.ahrq.gov/qual/nhdr06/nhdr06.htm
- Race, Ethnicity, and Healthcare-Policy Report
  http://www.kaiseredu.org/tutorials/REHealthcare/player.html

Race, Wealth, Housing, and You

Author: Piper Anderson

Grades: 8-12 +

Suggested Time Allowance: 90 minutes

Subject Areas: Social Sciences, History

Materials:
Pens
Paper
Newsprint
Markers
Crafts materials
Index cards
Computers

Overview: Students will discuss and reflect on their own relationship to wealth. Students will research and design a large timeline representing the racial wealth divide.

Vocabulary: Wealth, Equity

Objectives:
- To understand the institutional roots of the racial wealth divide in American as it relates to housing and wealth accumulation over generations.

Activities/Procedures:

1. <u>Warm-up: (10 minutes)</u>:
   This is a quick exercise to begin gathering perceptions about some the ideas we will be exploring in the session. Have the group stand in a circle and ask them to quickly respond to the following statements:

   > Money is…
   > Wealth is…
   > Housing is…
   > Power is…
   > Equality is…

   Allow each member of the entire group respond to the statement before going on to the next one. Encourage them to respond without hesitation saying the first thing that comes to mind.

2. <u>Concentric Circles: (15 minutes)</u>:

In this exercise students will share their own ideas about housing, homeownership, wealth. Split the group in half. Have one half form a circle and face out with their backs toward the inside of the circle. The second half of the group will then go and face someone stand in that circle forming a second outer circle.

Explain that you are going to pose a series of questions, which they will each have 60 seconds to respond to. After each pair has responded the students on the outer circle will move to one person to their left and respond to the next question with their new partner.
- Do you live in a house or apartment? What's the best part about living a house or an apartment?
- What does home ownership mean to you?
- What is wealth? Why is it important?
- How do people accumulate wealth?

Next, students will return to their seats. Ask for volunteers to share some of the things that they heard from others in the circle. Chart some of the common themes that come up in the sharing.

3. Race and Money: (20 minutes):
Explain that financial wealth is defined as economic assets. Assets are houses, other real estate, cash, stocks, bonds, pension funds, businesses and anything that can be liquidated or converted to cash. For many Americans their great financial asset is there home.

Do you think race plays a role in the ability to purchase a home or accumulate others kinds of wealth? Why or why not?

Explain that wealth is accumulated over generations. 80% of assets come from transfers from prior generations. What does that mean? Get responses from students.

Pose the questions:
- Raise your hand if you will inherit cash or other assets from your parents or grandparents?
- Raise your hand if your parents will pay for your or already have paid for your college tuition or will provide money to help you purchase your first car or home?
- Raise your hand if there is a home in your family that was purchased at least one generation before yours parents?

Explain that the ability pass assets to future generations is an important indicator of wealth, and the legacy of racial inequality in this country has barred many communities of color from being able purchase homes and accumulate wealth. This is known as the racial wealth divide. Next we will look at some of the programs and institutional policies that have created the racial wealth divide.

4. Race & Wealth Timeline Design (45 minutes):
   Explain to the group they are going to create a Race & Wealth Timeline in order to better understand the economic impact of government programs and historical events on families and communities.

   Before the session write each of the timeline moments listed below on index cards and distribute to students at random or by assignment. This list is merely a guide, you may opt to add and eliminate moments on the list as you deem appropriate.

   Next students will research their Timeline moment: Identifying what happened. What group of people was impacted by this incident? How were they impacted?

   After researching their timeline incident students will design an emblem symbolizing that event on the timeline that includes the title, a brief description of the who, what, how? Encourage them to be creative in crafting this symbol for the timeline.

   You may decide to map out a design for what the timeline will look like before the session considering size and materials and provide a guide for how large the timeline emblems should be.

   Timeline Moment:

   - 1849 Gold Rush Land Claims
   - Homestead Act
   - Indian Removal Act
   - Open Doors to European Immigration
   - Fugitive Slave Law
   - Mexican Land loss/Annexation of Mexican which later becomes state of Texas
   - Jim Crow Laws
   - 13th & 14th Amendments Passed
   - Plessey vs. Ferguson uphold separate but equal laws
   - Home Mortgage Reduction during WWI
   - Annexation of Hawaii, Puerto Rico, and Possession of the Philippines
   - 1913 Alien Land Laws
   - 1935 FHA Redlining
   - 1924 US Border Patrol
   - New Deal Federal Housing Loans, Social Security, Labor Rights
   - 1944 GI Bill
   - Indian Reorganization Act
   - Tribal Taxation
   - Farm loss due to USDA
   - Immigration Quotas
   - 1962 Cuban Refugee Assistance Act
   - 1964 Civil Rights
   - NAFTA

-1977Community Reinvestment Act
-1997 Tax cut for asset owners
- 1999-2009 Financial companies aggressively market subprime mortgages in communities predominately of color.

Extension Exercises:

1. Personal Essay on Wealth: Look at Race & Wealth Timeline created by your class and select one event that impacted your family's ability to accumulate wealth either privileging or disadvantaging you in wealth accumulation and write a personal essay detail the connections and how you feel it has impacted your family.

2. Digital Storytelling: This exercise requires a computer with video editing software like iMovie or Sony Vegas. Student's research their family's story learning about when they came to this country and the steps they took along the way to build a life here. Identify the key moments. Tell the story through images, music, and audio.

Interdisciplinary Connections:

Media/Technology: Digitize the Race & Wealth Timeline put it in a web format with hyperlinked pages, video, and images.

Economics/History: Students map their neighborhood's economic history from the 1950's to the present by identifying the median home price. Has it risen or fallen? What impact has that had on things like quality of schools, crime rate, access to public transportation, the kind of local businesses. Has the name of the neighborhood changed, demographic of the residence living there, etc.

Resources:

The Color of Wealth
United for a Fair Economy
Http://www.faireconomy.org

*Special thanks to Meizhu Liu from the Insight Center for Economic Development for information and feedback on this session.

"The system that was fashioned in order to exploit us [African-Americans] created an idea that this whole thing can happen. The notion of power is what supports it; it gives people the ability to say because of it I can lock you up, you won't get this job, or you will do this because of this kind of duress I can make in your life. It happens because of the implied power that comes from capitalism. So racism and white supremacy are byproducts, not the main problem. The primary contradiction in America is the fact that poor people don't have power. If we people had power, racism wouldn't matter because you couldn't do a damn thing to me. What informs racism is the power. It says 'not only do you believe that you are better than me, but because you do, and you've got these dudes backing you, you can make my life a little bit harder or a lot harder.' But if we were equal, if we had equal rights and justice, I wouldn't care if you hated me 'til death do us part. Then we good. That is the backing behind the ideology of white power and racism." *-M1, interview, 'Til the White Day is Done*

A Love Letter from Barbara Love

Dear Beloved:

This is "*critical*" work in which we are engaged, to express our full humanness by engaging with the world in order to change it, and to make it a more just world. Our aim to create a world where foolish notions about the ideology of race do not become predictors of life chances, life style, or life expectancy is, in fact, revolutionary. Thank you for your commitment to liberation. Thank you for your intention to make liberation happen in our lifetime.

The Founding People of these United States of America left us a great legacy: "That all 'humans' [men] are created equal; That they are endowed by their creator with certain inalienable rights, and that among these are life, liberty and the pursuit of happiness". These 'Founding People' aimed to create a society "of the people, by the people and for the people". They were hampered in what they could actually create by the times in which they lived and they ended up with something much more limited. They created a society where everyone could participate *if* they were landowning, literate, male, Christian, without disability, presumed heterosexual, and presumed to be white. That they were limited in what they could create does not diminish the significance of what they proposed: A society characterized by liberation.

Each new generation has done what it could to move this liberation agenda forward. It has come to us in our time to complete this work. We educators are in a unique position to move this agenda forward. It is small wonder that the battle for the control of the schools and the curriculum of the schools rages so fiercely. Schools and educators are a major force for socialization in our society. As educators, we provide possibilities for awareness for members of society; to either believe in the rightness of a system that produces results that are predictable by race for example, or to believe that such a system is in error and in need of change.

Our generation stands at a precipitous time in history, belonging as we do, to an historical era marked by extraordinary and unprecedented change. Capitalism thrashes in disarray in what could well be its death rattle. A new Black president of the United States of America is given the perhaps impossible task of saving it. Changes in the ecosystems of the world occur faster than we can predict and threaten a world order where those who have access to more resources feel free to expend them without regard for their impact on the world around them. Yet our generation has access to more resources with which to accomplish our historical task than any prior generation. The impact of human acts on Mother Earth is no longer possible to ignore. The World Wide Web, for instance, gives us access to information and means of communication that were unavailable to previous generations. Your classroom now resides inside four walls as well as outside those walls and spreads across the community, the region and the world.

What I offer in our unprecedented task is love. Love for this big wide wonderful world. Love for all the people in it. Love for you and for your commitment to change this world. Love for those who do not yet have a vision of liberation and are still limited by the boxes of history. Love for those who are either unable to look to the bright future characterized by liberation that we create together, or are unwilling to see the chaos coming if we fail. And yes, love for all of us who are arduously engaged in the work of creating a more just world.

I want you to remember that means are ends and the journey shapes the destination. People have mistakenly thought that "the ends justify the means" only to learn after the fact that whatever means they used infused the ends they were able to create. Likewise, people have mistakenly thought that the destination determined the route of the journey only to find out that where they arrived had been predetermined by the route they used to get there. Fortunately or unfortunately, this is unavoidable. This fusion of means and ends, journey and destination, seems, like gravity, to be a law of the universe. Take care to insure that love characterizes the means that you use. Be very sure that your journey has love at its core, for only in so doing can you insure that love accompanies you to as well as meets you at the destination.

Remember, my beloved, that those who are not aware of the power of love might scoff at your intention to wrap your journey to a just society in love. Those who oppose you might take your intention to teach with love as a sign of weakness. People who have tried very hard without seeing the results they hoped for might seek to pass along their discouragement and loss of hope to you. Fellow liberation workers might seek to gain energy from their anger and rage toward an unjust society and feel betrayed because you refuse to join them in their fury. It is true that rage and anger provides a certain kind of energy but it is energy that burns from the inside out. Energy fueled by rage and anger soon uses up and spits out those who wrap themselves in it. Rather than fear, or hopelessness or rage and anger, I urge you to hold love. Cultivate love. Teach with love.

For love and liberation,

Barbara Love

Dr. Love is a former teacher with an academic background in History and Political Science, and she has worked closely with schools and school systems throughout the U.S. and abroad. Her education background includes teacher education and staff development, curriculum development, and multicultural organizational development. She consults internationally on empowerment of women, especially women of color; has published widely on issues such as internalized racism, self-knowledge for social justice educators, building alliances for change, and black identity development; and is greatly sought after as a keynote speaker for NGO Forums and leadership conferences dealing with multicultural organizational development and social change.

Why are all the Black Kids Posting Together On MySpace? Racial Identity and Social Networking Sites

Author: Andrea Dre Domingue

Grades: 8-12+

Suggested Time Allowance: 90 minutes

Subject Areas: Technology

Materials:
Copies of "Social Networking Terminology"
Copies of "A Brief History of Social Network Sites"
Copies of "My Profile Worksheet"
Pens

Overview: The goal of this lesson is to have students gain a general understanding of the historical evolution of social networking sites and how these sites have influenced patterns of racial division among teenage and college users on the internet. Students will identify ways in which they construct personal and social identities online in comparable and different ways than in offline settings.

Vocabulary: Social Network/ing Sites

Objectives:
- Students will be able define and provide examples of social networking sites.
- Students will be able to describe critical incidents in history that have shaped the evolution of social networking sites, particularly as it relates to issues of race and access.
- Students will be able to identify the manner in which they construct their racial identity online and how it relates to their identity construction offline.

Activities/Procedures:
1. History of Online Social Networking Sites (45 minutes):
   Introduce the topic of online social networking and components of these sites as highlighted on the "Social Networking Terminology" handout on page 113.

   Note to Educators: While students may be familiar with these sites and terminology, it is still important to go over terms and definitions to create a common language to use throughout the lesson. This is also necessary to have students critically think about how these components function in regards to communication with others, identity expression, etc.

Following an overview of terminology, lead students through the "Brief History in Social Networking Timeline Activity." On the walls of the room, post the years covered in the timeline in chronological order. Next, randomly distribute major events within the timeline without the year in which they occurred. Instruct students that they are to arrange themselves on the various points in the timeline based on when they collectively think a particular event happened. Let students know that for some years there may be multiple events and these years are denoted with a number in parenthesis.

Once students are aligned on the timeline, have the person holding the earliest date read their fact aloud to the group. Confirm if that person is in the right position or ask them to move to the appropriate year they should be standing next to. Continue until the timeline is complete. Ask participants to take their seats and distribute the timeline handout. Engage students in a conversation about the activity:

- What new information did you learn?
- What information surprised you?
- What patterns can you identify from this timeline?
- How does this timeline relate to issues of race?
- What might be some reasons as to why race -specific sites such as BlackPlanet, MiGente and AsianAvenue were launched?
- Do you think there is a need for race-specific sites today? Why or why not?
- In your personal experience, do you find that different racial identities gravitate to different social networking sites? What possible explanation can you offer as to why this may or may not be the case?

Note to Educators: If the group number is larger than the number of events listed in the activity, additional events can be generated using the resources in the supplemental resources section. Also when engaging students about how race relates to social networking sites, have them think about the prevalence of race-specific sites, Facebook being initially exclusively available to Harvard University, access and cost of computers and internet, skill knowledge and literacy, privilege of time to be on the sites, etc.

2. Racial Identity and Social Network Sites (60 minutes):
For this next session, mention to students that they are going to further explore issues of race as it relates to social networking sites by looking at how personal and social identities are constructed. Remind students that personal identity refers to individual inner qualities and aspects a person has (hobbies, birth order, skills, favorite movies, etc.) while social identity refers to how someone would describe themselves in the

context of the socially determined categories such as race, gender religion/spirituality, etc.

Have students think about profiles on social network sites as they relate to personal and social identities. Next distribute and have them complete the My Profile Worksheet. Tell students that they can respond to any fields they want to with as little or as much information as they choose. Remind them that this is a chance for self-expression of who they are. Next have the students group themselves into pairs and each share aspects of their profiles.

Once students are done, refocus their attention to the front of the room. Remind students that in the Timeline Activity they were able to identify how race has had an influence on social network sites either by people opting to join race-specific online sites or how certain sites appealed and/or accessible to different users. To explore this deeper inform them that they are going look at the relationship between race and two specific sites: Facebook and MySpace.

On two flip chart papers write "MySpace" on one and "Facebook" on the other. Have students either write or verbally say what perceptions, messages or descriptors that come to mind when they think of these sites.

Note to Educators: It is suggested to get a sense before the lesson to know who is familiar with social networking sites in general as well as their familiarity with Facebook and MySpace. If students are unfamiliar with these sites, have them read the article following articles: "White Flight in Networked Publics? How Race and Class Shaped American Teen engagement with MySpace and Facebook" (for college level students) or have students listen to or read the transcript from the Morning Edition show episode "Facebook, MySpace Divides Along Social Lines," on National Public Radio. Both full references are listed in the supplemental resources section of this lesson.

- What are your reactions to argument of a racial and class divide among Facebook and MySpace users?
- Which sites are you apart of (if any) and what motivated you to join them?
- Was your race or the race of others a factor in determining which if any online sites you are associated with?
- How do you express yourself on social network sites?
- How do you express your race or ethnicity on your profile? Examples?
- How is your self-expression online different or similar than offline? Why or Why not?
- How much do you think about your racial identity when on social network sites?
- Think about your friends or contacts online. Do your friends tend to share or different racial identity than yourself?

- How does the racial identity of your online friends, differ if at all from offline friends.
- What kind of experiences have you had discussing race online? Examples?
- How does communication online about race differ if at all from communicating offline (advantages and disadvantages)?

Extension Activities:

1. Investigating Cyber or Online Racism (45 minutes):

   As a homework or an in-classroom assignment, ask students to go online to newspaper, magazine or media site and have them search and select an article that relates to the topic of race making sure the article has a comment feature where readers can post responses to the article. Some suggested topics could be affirmative housing, gentrification, immigration, interracial relationships, etc. Instruct the students to read the article carefully in its entirety, paying special attention to the type of site the article is from, what the article was about, and author's position. Next have students read the comments from readers about the article. Have students take notes on the positive and/or negative responses from readers making sure to note tone, word choice, arguments, and how readers may have interacted with other readers. As a large group have students share highlights on their findings and lead them in a discussion about online racism. Pose the following questions:
   - How would you describe cyber or online racism?
   - How is cyber or online racism different from racism offline?
   - What are some examples of cyber or online racism from your article investigation?
   - Why might people engage in cyber or online racism?
   - To what extent did the site of the article acknowledge or interrupt this racism?
   - What are some ways that you could respond or take action against cyber or online racism?
   - How can online media be used to promote anti-racism?

Interdisciplinary Connections:

Civics: For a further understanding, have students discuss and research how online racism relates to issues of free speech as well as investigating the degree to which online sites are legally required to response to online racism.

Supplemental Resources (Optional):

boyd, d. m. (Forthcoming). White flight in networked publics? How race and class shaped American teen engagement with MySpace and Facebook. In *Digital Race Anthology* (Eds. Lisa Nakamura and Peter Chow-White). Routledge. http://www.danah.org/papers/2009/WhiteFlightDraft3.pdf

boyd, d. m., & Ellison, N. B. (2007). Social network sites: Definition, history, and scholarship. *Journal of Computer-Mediated Communication, 13*(1), article 11. http://jcmc.indiana.edu/vol13/issue1/boyd.ellison.html

Fairlie, Robert W. (2004). "Race and the Digital Divide," *Contributions to Economic Analysis & Policy*: Vol. 3 : Iss. 1, Article 15. Available at: http://www.bepress.com/bejeap/contributions/vol3/iss1/art15

Hargittai, E. (2007). Whose space?: Differences among users and non-users of social network sites. *Journal of Computer--Mediated Communication*, *13*(1), article 14. http://jcmc.indiana.edu/vol13/issue1/hargittai.html

Nakamura, L. (2002).*Cybertypes: Race, ethnicity, and identity on the internet*. London: Routledge.

Sydell, L. (2009, October 21). Morning Edition. *Facebook, MySpace divides along social lines*. Podcast from retrieved from NPR: from http://www.npr.org/templates/story/story.php?storyId=113974893

Social Networking Terminology

Social Network Sites or Social Networking Sites
Refers to internet-based sites where individuals are able to create profiles that depict aspects of themselves and visibly identifies connections one with others individuals, groups or entities that also use the site. While profiles and connections can vary in degree to which they are visible to other users, the general purpose of these sites is to serve as tool to help individuals find and stay in contact with others in which they have a preexisting relationship or to make new connections. Typically these terms are interchangeable, but some argue that in order to use the word "networking" requires an active pursuit of connecting with individuals that one has not already had an existing relationship with.
Examples: Friendster, MySpace, Facebook, LiveJournal, Blogger, LinkedIn, Twitter, etc.

Profiles
A way of identifying one's self on a social network site. Typical components include: name , picture, interests/hobbies, affiliations, quotes, synopsis of self (about me), and synopsis of who they are looking to interact with (who I want to meet), geographic location, birthday, contact information (email, phone, etc.) , religion, education, work, dating status, etc. (Important to mention that sites like MySpace and Facebook have scripts and application to help users change what fields are created or removed, example gender identity.

Friends/Contacts/Fans
Individuals a user is connected to or has a relationship with on a particular site. Users become friends by mutually agreeing to be connected to one another. General, most social networking sites have a feature where users can be found by searching by name, location, networks, or other criterion.

Privacy- the degree to which others can see one's profile in full or aspects of profile. Can be a general setting or a setting specific to individuals or groups of people.

Groups-a space where people come together over common interests, beliefs, involvement, etc.

Networks
Categories usually generated by social network sites. These categories are used to not only allow users to identify affiliations but also serve as a way of connecting the user to others who also selected the same category. Examples: schools, companies, professional associations, cities, etc.

Posts
Items that that users can place on their own or other's profile. Items include, pictures/photo albums, web links, written statements, videos, notes, etc.

Comments, Messages & Chat
Ways of communicating with users on a particular site. Comments are response to items that are posted on a person's profile. Messages are private or semi-private ways of communicating with others that will not appear on individual's profile. Chat is a feature that allows users to communicate with each other in real-time through an instant messaging.

A Brief History of Social Network Sites

1993	America Online (AOL) becomes widely available after only being initially compatible for Mac computers. An internet-service provider, this site also allowed users were able to create profiles, email, join communities, etc.
1995	Classmates.com launched, a site for people to connect with past classmates from high school.
1997	SixDegrees.com launched. Argued as the first social network site and largely based on the pop culture theory that people are connected to each other within six degrees. This site eventually closed in 2000.
1999	LiveJournal launched, online journaling and community.
1999	BlackPlanet & AsianAvenue launched. Sites specifically launched for African Americans and Asian Americans.
2000	MiGente launched. A site specifically created for those who identify as Latino.
2002	Friendster launched. Premise of the site was to highlight true bonds and connections between people (friendships)
2003	LinkedIn launched. A site whose main purpose was to show professional connections and credentials.
2003	MySpace launched. Initially this site appealed to independent musicians, namely rock and hip-hop, as a way to widely market their groups. Site gained interests from teenagers and young adults located in urban settings. Due to limited privacy settings, mainstream media described it as "dangerous" or "unsafe" for teen users.
2003	Facebook launched. Initially this site was only accessible to those affiliated with Harvard University as way to connect its students. Later that year, the site became available to other Ivy League schools.
2004	Facebook open to those at all universities and individuals with an email address ending with .edu.
2004	Orkut launched. Created by Google.
2005	Facebook begins becoming available to high schools.
2005	AsianAvenue and BlackPlanet relaunches.
2005	YouTube launches. A site that allows users to upload and comment on online videos.
2006	Facebook becomes available to all people.
2006	Twitter is launched. A micro-blogging site that allows users to only post messages that are 140 characters maximum.

Adapted from:

boyd, d. m., & Ellison, N. B. (2007). Social network sites: Definition, history, and scholarship. *Journal of Computer-Mediated Communication, 13*(1), article 11. http://jcmc.indiana.edu/vol13/issue1/boyd.ellison.html

Nickson, C. (2009, January 21). *The history of social networking. Retrieved from* http://www.digitaltrends.com/features/the-history-of-social-networking/

Name

Picture

Hometown/Location:

School:

Major/favorite subject:

Religion/Spirituality:

Friends

Groups

Activities

Interests

Favorites Music

Favorite TV Shows or Movies

About Me

Who I am Looking to Meet

111

Race and the Media:
Our Legacy is What We Leave Behind

Author: Samantha Shapses Wertheim

Grades: 8-12+

Suggested Time Allowance: Approximately 120 minutes

Subject Areas: Behavior Studies, Anthropology, Sociology, Communication, Media Studies, Critical Thinking

Materials:
A popular magazine
Short media clips from: a nightly news show, a sitcom, and a music video
Ethnographic question sheet
Access to the internet or pre-recorded videos

Overview: In this lesson students will begin to critically examine what cultural dynamics regarding race are reflected through various forms of media through the lens of cultural anthropology and ethnographic studies. Students will use their own observations to determine the salient values regarding Race in American society.

Vocabulary: media, ethnography

Objectives:
- To introduce students to the following areas of study and terms: Cultural Anthropology, Culture, Media, Ethnography, Race.
- To collectively brainstorm questions that will assist in learning about the value system of a culture.
- To apply those questions to popular media.
- To process the picture of American society that the media portrays.
- To reflect upon one's personal experience in this exercise.
- To innovate new ways of promoting positive societal values through media.

Activities/Procedures:

1. Definitions (35 minutes)

    To begin the session, state the overall goal: Today we will be using the lens of cultural anthropology to discuss Race and the Media. You will have an opportunity to reflect on this process, and innovate new ways of promoting equity among races in the media. (5 minutes)

Write the following words on large post-it papers or board: Cultural Anthropology, Culture, Media, Ethnography and Race. Give each student a marker, and have them write down words or definitions that that they associate with these words. (10 minutes)

When the students have finished hand out the list of definitions of the words. Together go through all of the words, after reading what has been written on the paper, ask a student to read the definition out loud to the group. Continue to do this for each of the words. (20 minutes)

Culture	The customs, arts, social institutions, and achievements of a particular nation, people, or other social group ("Merriam-Webster Dictionary")
Anthropology	The science of human beings; *especially*: the study of human beings and their ancestors through time and space and in relation to physical character, environmental and social relations, and culture ("Merriam-Webster Dictionary")
Cultural Anthropology	Anthropology that deals with human culture especially with respect to social structure, language, law, politics, religion, magic, art, and technology ("Merriam-Webster Dictionary")
Ethnography	The study and systematic recording of human cultures *Media*: the main means of mass communication (esp. television, radio, newspapers, and the Internet) regarded collectively ("Merriam-Webster Dictionary")
Media	The main means of mass communication (esp. television, radio, newspapers, and the Internet) regarded collectively ("Merriam-Webster Dictionary")
Race	A social construct that artificially divides people into distinct groups based on characteristics such as physical appearance (particularly skin color), ancestral heritage, cultural affiliation or history, ethnic classification, and/or the social, economic, and political needs of a society at a given period of time. Scientists agree that there is no biological or genetic basis for racial categories. (Adams, Bell and Griffin, 2007)

2. Why are we discussing ethnography? (5 minutes)
   • Ethnography is a means of collecting unbiased research about community, culture or people.

113

- It is the goal of the ethnography to be open-ended and unbiased. To create a picture of a culture without stereotypes.
- We are now going to attempt to look at media with an unbiased eye.

Extension Activity (20 minutes)
Have students conduct a mini-research project by using popular television shows. Have students choose the top 4-6 mainstream television networks. Then ask students to create a list of which shows air on those networks during primetime viewing hours. After students have gathered the names of the shows and the networks they appear on, the student should create a racial inventory of the casts. Students can do this by watching the TV show and recording their perception of the racial identities of the characters or by visiting the web sites for the various shows. All '"assumptions" about racial identities should be cross-referenced by "googling" the actors to confirm how they identity. The results of this research should be shared in a presentation to the larger group.

3. Brainstorming questions: (15 minutes)
   Propose the following question and record all answers up on the board:
   What questions should we ask when attempting to learn about a society? Since we are focusing on race and the media what questions should we ask regarding race?

   Write all questions on the board. Sample questions are provided below:
   - How are white people characterized in the media?
   - How are people of color characterized in the media?
   - What adjectives can you use to describe people of different races? Asian? Latino? White? Black/African American? Multi-racial? Southeast Asian? (Feel free to ask the students for suggestions of different races)
   - What items are important to people of different races?
   - How frequently do you see people of different races?
   - How do different races interact? Do they interact with each other?
   - What types of language do people use? Does it differ depending upon what race they are?
   - What is the power dynamic between different races?
   - What is the power dynamic of people in general?
   - How do different races interact with their environment?
   - What environments are people of different races surrounded in?
   - What activities do people of different races enjoy participating in? Which do they not enjoy?
   - Are men and women of different races treated differently? If so, how?
   - Any additional questions...

4. Set the tone (40 minutes)
   Now explain to the students that you would like them to pretend that they are all cultural anthropologists interested in investigating this certain culture, and that you will provide each group with an 'artifact' to assess and gather information from. Ask

them to do their best to remain unbiased and answer the questions that you have brainstormed. (3 minutes)

Divide the group into four groups and provide: (5 minutes)
Note to Educators: Examples of these clips can be found at www.jlovecalderon.com, or you can utilize your own clips

Group One: Nightly News Clip
Group Two: Music Video
Group Three: Popular Magazine
Group Four: Sit-Com Clip

Instruct the students to write down on a large paper what they 'discovered' about their culture from their artifact. When they have completed it hang up each paper and ask the students to walk around and read what the other groups wrote in regards to their item. (20 minutes to write, 10 minutes to view)

5. Processing (20 minutes)
   Note to educators: Processing can be done as a group, or given as a worksheet for individuals, and then asked to volunteer to share answers to their questions.

   Propose the following questions to process this activity, you can list the questions on the board or simply read them out loud.

   - What did you discover that surprised you?
   - What did not surprise you?
   - How did it feel to act as an unbiased anthropologist? Was this difficult or easy?
   - What factors affect the way that people recognize race in the media?

   The last question can be used in the group processing or given as a reflection activity to take home:

   How does my social identity (race, religion, class, gender, sexuality etc.) affect the way I recognize race in the media?

Extension Activity:
1. Steps towards liberation (25 min)
   Explain to the students that for the last part of the exercise you would like to challenge them to be creative and create 'artifacts' that reflect a race in the media in a positive and equitable light. Ask the students to return to their original groups and use the following questions to design their 'artifact'
   - What would you change about this article to make it more equitable?
   - What would it look like?
   - What would it sound like?

- What values would it reflect?
- Who would it be designed for?
- Who would have access to it?

Ask the group to present their 'new artifact' to the larger group when they are finished.

6. <u>Take Aways / Conclusion (5 min)</u>
   To close, ask the students to share a take away; a new insight or idea that they will take with them from this exercise.

Interdisciplinary Connections:

Mathematics: Tracking is the action of taking notice without judgment the occurrence of various activities or actions. For example one might track, how many times a man allows women to exit first. Explain to the students what tracking is and ask them to 'track' one activity in the media for a full day, tallying all instances on a piece of paper.

For example:

How many times today did I see a white person on a sitcom? How many times did I see a person of color on a sitcom?

When the students have the number answers for these questions ask them to put those numbers in to percentages to calculate the percentage of times a white person appears on television, versus the percentage of time a person of color appears on a sit-com. You can also ask the students to create a number of different types of graphs using this data as well.

Works Cited

Adams, M., Bell, L. A., & Griffin, P. (2007). *Teaching for diversity and social justice* (2nd ed.). New York: Routledge.

Anthropology. (2010). In *Merriam-Webster Online Dictionary*. Retrieved January 24, 2010, from http://www.merriam-webster.com/dictionary/anthropology

Cultural anthropology. (2010). In *Merriam-Webster Online Dictionary*. Retrieved January 24, 2010, from http://www.merriam-webster.com/dictionary/cultural anthropology.

Ethnography. (2010). In *Merriam-Webster Online Dictionary*. Retrieved January 24, 2010, from http://www.merriam-webster.com/dictionary/ethnography

Media. (2010). In *Merriam-Webster Online Dictionary*. Retrieved January 24, 2010, from http://www.merriam-webster.com/dictionary/media

A Love Letter from Ariel Luckey

ID Check by Ariel Luckey © 2009

I am a blue-eyed devil, peckawood, and country cracker
Red neck, white trash, and urban wannabe rapper
I am the man who's got the God complex
Pimping privilege from class, skin color, and sex
I am the president, the pope, and the cop on your block
I'm the banker buying stock in selling bullets and glocks

This is an ID check
Like a rope around your neck
Better know who you are
When death calls collect

This is an ID check
Like the border patrol
But this is not for your country
This is for your soul
I am the great great great grandchild of the Mayflower
Gave thanks to God for smallpox so I could take power
I'm the great great grandchild of broken treaties
Inheritor of racial slurs spoken freely
I'm the great grandchild of BIA and Homestead Act
I shot Wounded Knee, stabbed Crazy Horse in the back
I'm the grandchild of Jim Crow and burning crosses
I yelled for a lynching, then brought my children to watch it
I'm the child of GI Bill, white affirmative action
Got promotions and jobs reserved for Anglo-Saxons
I am the father of Katrina and government neglect
This is a race roll call
This is an ID check

I am President Andrew Johnson, I took your 40 acres away
I am William Simmons, I led the KKK
I am Senator Joe McCarthy, I blacklisted the nation
I am Governor Orval Faubus, I blocked integration
I am Roy Bryant and J.W. Milam
I murdered Emmett Till and then denied that I killed him
I'm Lawrence Brewer, John King, and Shawn Allen Berry
Dragged James Byrd to his death in a black cemetery
I am Michael Brown, I directed FEMA

I am Walter Reed, I prosecuted 6 from Jena
I am Bill O'Reilly, I spew hate everyday
I am George W. Bush, what else do I need to say

This is an ID check
Like airport security
The real terrorism
State of emergency

This is an ID check
Like the border patrol
But this is not for your country
This is for your soul

I'm a 12th generation illegal immigrant
My family sold our culture as an economic stimulant
I have stolen the language of West African griots
Sampled the stand up bass of standard jazz trios
I have eaten the heart beatin of the boogie down Bronx
Carved a new ivory tower out of elephant tusk ankhs
I appropriate your culture cause I sold my roots
Got my hair did in corn rows, sport Timberland boots
I wear a bindi on my forehead, Che's face on my chest
I wave sage and an eagle feather and call this space blessed
I got a Chinese character tattooed on my arm
Rock an Om necklace as a good luck charm
I am Wonder Bread, I am the Melting Pot
I buy my coolness at the mall cause that's what I've been taught
I'm a Pilgrim, a Cowboy, All-American athlete
I am Elvis, Kenny G, Vanilla Ice, and Backstreet

This is an ID check
This is a shattered mirror
This is the voice of whitey
This is the psyche of fear

This is an ID check
Like the border patrol
But this is not for your country
This is for your soul

I walk on red carpet sewn in maquiladoras
I pimp the stock market with the ruling class employers
I make a living from your dying, I am free trade
I'm the law that says IMF loan interest gets paid

I am middle class white flight and suburbanization
I'm a yuppie drinking latte, Starbucks gentrification
I live in Sundown towns and feast on strange fruit
I get paid for every ghetto youth the army recruits
I am the air you breathe, the water you drink
I'm the hegemony underneath the way you think
I am white supremacy and patriotism
I am the private profits made from public prisons
I'm the cop in your head, I am COINTELPRO
I'm the non-profit industrial complex's cash flow
I am white collar crime and corporate subsidies
I spit dirty white lies, I'm Fox news publishing
I'm Cheney's Energy Task Force getting together
I'm the smoking gun, I am Enron's paper shredder
I'm a Blackwater mercenary paid by your taxes
I'm a federal bail out to Wall Street while the economy collapses
I am the stars and stripes, huh, united we stand
I'm the great white hope, I am superman

This is an ID check
Like 3 o'clock road block
This is psychotherapy
By electric shock

This is an ID check
Like the border patrol
But this is not for my country
This is for my soul

cause
I am also Robert Carter, I freed 500 of my slaves
I'm Supreme Court Justice John Jay, I ruled against racist ways
I am Preacher John Woolman, I'm a Quaker Abolitionist
I'm Henry David Thoreau, I wrote Civil Disobedience
I am John Brown, I raided Harper's Ferry
I'm Ralph Waldo Emerson, a poet revolutionary
I am Mark Twain, I protested imperialism in the Philippines
I am Albert Einstein, I raised my voice against lynching
I am Myles Horton, I founded Highlander Center's popular education
I'm Abraham Joshua Heschel, Marching with Dr. King my feet were praying
I am Andrew Goodman and Michael Schwerner
I campaigned for justice in the Freedom Summer
I am Bill Ayers, I forecast the Weather Underground
I'm Jack Junebug Boykin, I led the Young Patriots in Chicago's Uptown
I am Howard Zinn, I wrote the People's History

I am Noam Chomsky, I drop knowledge on society
I am Paul Kivel, I wrote Uprooting Racism
I am Tim Wise, I speak truth across the nation
I'm the push for racial justice
I am freedom on the rise
I am the possibility
in my son's blue eyes

This is an ID check
like the border patrol
but this is not for our country
this is for our soul

Note: While this poem is specifically about white men and the legacy of white male racism and resistance in the united states, I must acknowledge the contributions of white women anti-racist activists, such as Virginia Durr, Anne Braden, Linda Evans, and Mab Segrest, among many others, who have played critical roles in the movements for racial justice.

Dear Father,

I want to share with you a story. It is a love story. Not the sweet romantic butterfly kiss kind of love, though that also makes good stories. This is a story of a love of people, and of justice. Actually, it is several stories that make one.

When I was about 6 years old, your mother, you, and I were walking down to the Oakland Rose Garden to play catch among the flowers. I was laughing and running ahead when I fell and scraped my knee on the sidewalk. I promptly burst into tears. Grandma flashed red and scolded me. "Stop crying! You're a big boy now." "No, it's okay," you said, "It's okay to cry," as you hugged me close and brushed off my knee. In those simple words, and the example you lived that demonstrated them, you taught me one of the most important things about being a healthy human being. It is essential to open my heart to life's wide range of emotion: to feel and express my pain and vulnerability, and that of others. For a white man in this culture, this is revolutionary, and takes daily practice.

Four years later, driving me to a doctor's appointment, you hand me a children's book to read in the car. "What is this?" I ask. The book looks like it's for toddlers. "Just read it," you say, "and tell me if you notice anything." It's about different things people do for a living. Some people are doctors. Others are carpenters. Still others bake bread. "Okay, I read it." "What did you notice?" "Um, nothing." "What did you notice about the people?" "They were doing different things?" "Yeah, and what kind of people are they?" "I don't know, just normal people." "Look again." I scan through the book, trying to figure it out. "I don't know. What about the people?" "They're all white," you say calmly. And it slowly dawns on me, a steady brightening of awareness. I never thought about "reading" a book like that before. Even though many of my classmates speak Arabic, Spanish, Mandarin, Farsi, and Amharic at home; even though many of our neighbors come from countries all over the world; even though many of the doctors, carpenters, and bakers in my community are people of color; I still saw a book of only white people as so normal

that I didn't even notice it. "That's part of how racism works," you say. "It makes people of color and their contributions invisible." And then we park the car and walk over to the doctor's office.

One afternoon you pick me up from high school and we head to the BART train station to ride under the Oakland hills to the suburbs beyond. We carry two boxes of colorful flyers that boldly pronounce the name of the grassroots group you have been organizing with: Angry White Men *for* Affirmative Action. Drawing attention to the long legacy of affirmative action programs that exclusively benefited white men, you, along with several hundred other progressive white men, have been campaigning against Proposition 209. Prop 209 would end all affirmative action programs, many which now benefit white women and people of color, in the state of California. For two hours we stand outside a BART station, passing out flyers and talking to commuters about how affirmative action seeks to mitigate the many barriers to equal education still imposed by institutional racism and sexism. On the way home, we talk about the campaign, people's responses to the flyers, and the politics of being a white ally to people of color.

In small everyday ways and larger breakthrough moments, you taught me to love people, and justice. You taught me about compassion, critical thinking, and action. Your book, *Uprooting Racism: How White People Can Work for Racial Justice*, taught me a lot about being a white ally. But your example and your fatherhood taught me so much more.

Love,

Ariel

Dear Son,

I want to share with you a story. It is a love story. Not the sweet romantic butterfly kiss kind of love, though that also makes good stories. This is a story of a love of people, and of justice. Actually, it is several stories that make one.

On the first day of school in fourth grade I sat next to a boy who had recently arrived from Ethiopia. He lived with his Mom and four other relatives in a two-bedroom apartment two blocks from my house. We quickly became best friends. We walked to and from school together everyday. We played together after school and had sleepovers on the weekends. We developed a deep bond of friendship and I grew to love him dearly. He could speak English well and had quickly adapted to life and culture in the States, but he had joined our school after they taught students basic reading skills and he had dyslexia. He was a young black boy in an Oakland public school who didn't know how to read. While our teacher failed him and made him repeat the fourth grade, there was no one who took the time to actually teach him to read. Year after year he slipped through the cracks, and I learned that a young black man graduating high school with a fourth grade reading level was no big deal to the teachers and administrators in the school system. It was

business as usual to them, but it angered me deeply. Love for my friend and my desire for him to have an equal opportunity to get an education sparked my commitment to racial justice.

Many years later, while facilitating a diversity training with climate change activists, focusing on how to build the organization's capacity to address racism internally and within the movement, I led the group through the Forum Theater process developed by Brazilian actor Augusto Boal. Forum Theater uses theatrical techniques to walk a group of people through a collective strategizing session on how to solve a common problem. The first step is to create a short scene that demonstrates the problem. Then invite members of the audience to one by one enter the scene and "act out" potential solutions. After each solution is tried, the group reflects on its effectiveness and applicability in real life. We created a scene that depicted an interpersonal act of racism that no one interrupted. Instead of just talking about how we should all interrupt racism, participants have to actually get out of their seats and use their bodies and voices to *practice* interrupting racism.

Even in a supportive environment with a hypothetical theater exercise, this is not easy to do. Let alone in real life! The typical responses to interpersonal acts of racism are either to do nothing and feel bad about it, or to lash out and attack the person who committed the act. Neither is effective. Doing this work and reflecting on my own life, I have found that challenging family members and others we love closely is even more difficult. Of course, this only makes it more important to do. A third possible response is assertive and challenging engagement grounded in love and compassion, one much more likely to result in dialogue and a movement towards racial justice. And like any skill set it takes intention, commitment, and practice to develop. It also takes love, sometimes tough love, for people, and for justice.

One evening a few months ago you and I were snuggling in bed while I read your bedtime story. Your Mama was out with a friend for dinner. As I finished the story we heard our front door open and someone come inside. You immediately bounced out of bed and ran into the living room to see who it was. "Who is it?" I called. You ran back to your room, "Mama and the brown guy." "The brown guy" is an old and close friend of ours, one you know well and love. "You silly," I say, "that's our friend." And I say his name. I know you know his name. And you are noticing and articulating difference in skin color. At four years old you are already learning about race and our conversations are just beginning. As you grow up and grapple with who you are, your role in community, and your relationship to racism, I am here for you; to support and challenge you, and to be challenged by you; to help you learn about compassion, critical thinking, and action; to stand with you for racial justice, and love.

Love,

Ariel

Born and raised in Oakland, California, Ariel Luckey is a son, brother, and father whose community and performance work dances in the crossroads of education, art, & activism. Named a "Visionary" by Utne Reader, Ariel performs his hip hop theater solo show, Free Land, *in theaters, classrooms, and conferences across the country. He recently published his first book, a collection of poetry and lyrics, entitled* Searching For White Folk Soul.

Criminal Justice/Racial Injustice

Author: Piper Anderson

Grades: 8-12+

Suggested Time Allowance: 90 minutes

Subject Areas: History, Political Science, Civics

Materials:
Pens
Paper
Newsprint
Markers

Overview: This lesson provides students with the opportunity to explore the ways in which racism impacts the criminal justice system.

Vocabulary: incarceration

Objectives:
- Students will reflect on the impact that racial disparities in the criminal justice system has on communities and families.

Activities/Procedures:
1. Graffiti Board: (15 minutes)
   Before students arrive hang a large sheet of newsprint on the wall and write at the top: who is impacted by the criminal justice system?

   Provide students with markers and allow them to chart their own responses to this question on the newsprint. Encourage them to think beyond justice individuals to groups, institutions, cultural impact, etc.

   After everyone has written their responses everyone should step back and look at what has been written. Together, point out common themes, words, or phrases that interest or surprise you.

2. Criminal Justice/Racial Injustice: (15 minutes)
   Share the following statistics with the group:
   > More than 70% of the prison population is Black and Latino
   > For Black men in their twenties every 1 in 8 is in prison or jail.

The Sentencing Project has found that the over representation of African Americans and Latinos in prisons is not simply the result of greater criminal activity in those communities:

The cause of racial disparities in include:
Racial profiling of communities of color by law enforcement
Lack of affordable effective legal counsel
Laws that target low level drug offenders

For example: Under New York State's Rockefeller Drug Law offenders carrying two ounces of crack cocaine, considered a poor mans drug, receive a mandatory 15 years to life prison sentence. One would have to carry twice as much pure cocaine to receive the same sentence. Laws like these unfairly target poorer drug users from Black and Latino communities.

It may be more useful to break this information up and chart it for the group to read together. Take a moment to respond to any questions the group may have about the information given before moving on.

3. Picture the Impact: (40 minutes)
Divide student into small groups of 4-5. What are your initial reactions to the statistics and information on the criminal justice system?

Give groups about five minutes for reflection. Next have the groups create a still image in response to the question: What impact does the racial disparities in the criminal justice system have on families and communities?

Explain that a still image is a snap shot or picture, no movement and no speaking, just a picture to capture a moment. Give them about 10-15 minutes to create their image.

Groups will present images. Ask them to show their image without explaining it first, they can talk about their image in the large group discussion after everyone has presented. While the image is held ask the audience: What do you see? Popcorn-style get responses from several volunteers.

4. Reflection: (10-15 minutes)
In the large group reflect on what the group witnessed in the images.

1. What were some of themes you saw in the images presented?
2. What did the images say about families and communities are impacted by the criminal justice system?

Extension Activities:
1. Write an op-ed about racial disparities in incarceration and submit it to your local paper.

2. Write a play about a family who is dealing with the lost of a love one to the criminal justice system.

Interdisciplinary Connection:
Economics: Identify what the cost of incarceration is in your state compared to the cost of public education. Where does your state invest its money? What are consequences for young people in your state?

Political Science: Research criminal justice policy then create a mantle of the experts where individual represent policy representatives making a case for changes in the criminal justice system

Resources:
The Sentencing Project
http://www.sentencingproject.org

"There are not many people I can talk about my true feelings with, so I'm afraid I must burden them with you. As they led me off the bus, I was acutely aware of the coldness of my new surroundings that I would call home for the next 16 years. As I was shuffled in with the other inmates, all of us feeling like animals, I began contemplating how I would maintain my sanity and stay alive. At that same moment, a fly perched itself proudly on my shoulder. With my hands and feet shackled with steel handcuffs, I remained powerless, unable to do the simplest of all tasks, like brushing off a fly. At that moment, I felt the little fly had conquered me, had conquered my manhood. And that, my friend, is the clearest way I can describe what it feels like to have your freedom taken from you. Pray for me."

-A letter by formerly incarcerated artist Jay Mason, published in That White Girl *by* JLove

---

Zero Tolerance for the School to Prison Pipeline

Author: Piper Anderson

Grades: 8-12+

Suggested Time Allowance: 90 minutes

Subject Areas: Social Sciences

Materials:
Pens
Paper
Newsprint
Markers
Print outs of the Alternative Disciplinary Code exercise

Overview: Students share their experiences with Zero Tolerance Policies. Students will create a disciplinary code, which will serve as an alternative to zero tolerance policies.

Vocabulary: prison pipeline, tolerance

Objectives:
- Participants will understand what the school to prison pipeline is, and who is affected by it and explore alternatives.

Activities/Procedures:
1. <u>What is Zero Tolerance? (15 minutes)</u>
   On newsprint begin a web with the word Zero Tolerance inside it. What does zero tolerance mean to you? What words, images, ideas come to mind when you see this word?

   If you're presenting this in a school with a zero tolerance policy ask the students for their reactions to it. Is it fair? Does it keep students safe? (If this workshop is not in school survey the group to see who goes to a school with a zero tolerance policy).

2. <u>Group Sharing: (10 minutes)</u>
   In small groups of 3-4 ask students to share with each other their own experiences with zero tolerance policies or witnessing their policies in action in their schools.
   What do zero tolerance policies look like?
   Who is most often affected by zero tolerance policies?
   How do these policies impact student experiences of school?

Ask for members of each group to report back some of what was discussed.

If it hasn't already been stated share with the group that the biggest consequences of zero tolerance policies are student expulsion and repeated suspension and that the group most impacted by these policies are African American students.

When students are expelled or repeatedly suspended from school they are more like to drop out of school and become incarcerated. Because of zero tolerance policies a school to prison pipeline has been formed.

3. <u>What is the school to prison pipeline? (10 minutes)</u>

    Ask for a volunteer to read the following definition:

    The School to Prison Pipeline (STPP) is a nationwide system of local, state, and federal education and public safety policies that pushes students out of school and into the criminal justice system. The system disproportionately targets youth of color and youth with disabilities. Inequities in areas such as school discipline, policing practices, high-stakes testing, wealth and healthcare distribution, school "grading" systems, and the prison-industrial complex all contribute to the Pipeline. (Source: NYCLU)

    Get initial reactions to this statement: do you feel school disciplinary policies can push students into the prison system? How?

4. <u>What's the Alternative? (45 minutes)</u>
    Divide students into groups of 4-5. Give each group their instructions on a print out that reads:

    You are a student leadership council who has been asked to draft a disciplinary code for the school as an alternative to the zero tolerance policy, which has led to an overrepresentation of African American and Latino youth in suspension.

    - How can you keep students safe while also finding ways to prevent unnecessary suspension and expulsion for students of color?
    - How can disciplinary issues be addressed in school by Administrators, Students, and Teachers?
    - How can students play a key role in the creation of disciplinary policies in school?

    Chart your disciplinary code and prepare to share with the larger group.

Extension Activities:
1. Share your disciplinary policy with administrators at your school ask them to consider implementing or at least discussing them with the students.

Interdisciplinary Connections:
Fine Arts: Create a visual representation of the school to prison pipeline

Language Arts: Research a news story about a young person expelled from school because of zero tolerance policies. Put yourself in their shoes and write a story from that student's perspective.

Resources:
Dismantling the School to Prison Pipeline
http://www.naacpldf.org/content/pdf/pipeline/Dismantling_the_School_to_Prison_Pipeli ne.pdf

Works Cited
Jackson, J. L. (2001). *Zero Tolerance: Resisting the Drive for Punishment.* New York: New Press.

Race and Affirmative Action

Author: Tanesha Barnes

Grades: 8-12+

Suggested Time Allowance: 90 minutes

Subject Areas: Civics, History

Materials:
Myths and Facts about Affirmative Action Handout
Blackboard or Newsprint
Markers

Overview: In this lesson students will explore the relationship between affirmative action and white privilege. In addition, students will review six popular myths about affirmative action and corresponding facts that dispel their truths.

Vocabulary: Privilege, Affirmative Action

Objectives:
- To learn the first time that the term affirmative action is used in U.S. laws.
- To introduce students to the term privilege and discuss its relationship with affirmative action.
- To provide students with a list of common myths about affirmative action and their truths.

Activities/Procedures:
1. <u>Warm-Up (10 minutes):</u> Read the following quote to students
"We don't see outside of this particular kind of box, you know, we more accept our reality as one with a glass ceiling. And that ceiling is racism. And everywhere we go they even developed terminology around it, institutional racism, and factions of it, but the reason why it can happen that way is because it has permeated our society and said these are the unwritten rules that guide humanity."

Ask students to reflect on this interview for 'Til the White Day is Done from M1, one of the member's of the hip-hop duo Dead Prez and in particular what are the "unwritten rules" that they think M1 is referring to in this passage.

2. <u>History of Affirmative Action Term Activity (15 minutes):</u> Write the following quote on newsprint or on the blackboard for students to see.

"The contractor will not discriminate against any employee or applicant for employment because of race, creed, color, or national origin. The contractor will take

130

affirmative action to ensure that applicants are employed, and that employees are treated during employment, without regard to their race, creed, color, or national origin. Such action shall include, but not be limited to, the following: employment, upgrading, demotion or transfer; recruitment or recruitment advertising; layoff or termination; rates of pay or other forms of compensation; and selection for training, including apprenticeship. The contractor agrees to post in conspicuous places, available to employees and applicants for employment, notices to be provided by the contracting officer setting forth the provisions of this nondiscrimination clause."
- President John F. Kennedy's Executive Order 10925 (1961)
"Executive Order 10925 - Establishing The President's Committee on Equal Employment Opportunity". The American Presidency Project. Retrieved 2010-01-23. http://www.presidency.ucsb.edu/ws/index.php?pid=58863.

Inform students that this is the first time that the term affirmative action entered our vocabulary as a nation in our written laws. Ask students to share their initial thoughts and reactions to the above statement. What major historical events were taking place during the time that President Kennedy wrote Executive Order 10925? What impact do you believe these events had on President Kennedy's decision to write Executive Order 10925, if any?

3. Definitions Activity (25 minutes): Provide definitions for the word privilege to students and ask them to provide you with examples of ways that white people have privilege in our society. Ask students to try not to think about individual benefits but institutional benefits such as health care, representation in the media, etc. Write the word privilege on the blackboard or on newsprint and draw a line making two columns, for now do not write the title of the second column. Write the examples that students provide in the privilege column.

Privilege: unearned access to resources only readily available to some people as a result of their advantaged social group membership.

After students have given you five examples of white privilege, provide them with the definition for affirmative action. At this time you should also write the affirmative action as the title for the second column. Ask students to think of ways that affirmative action policies can help to balance some of the unearned benefits that white people receive.

Affirmative Action: any measure, beyond simple termination of a discriminatory practice, that permits the consideration of race, national origin, sex, or disability, along with other criteria, and which is adopted to provide opportunities to a class of qualified individuals who have either historically or actually been denied those opportunities and/or to prevent the recurrence of discrimination in the future.

Now that both columns are complete, ask students to share their thoughts on the relationship between white privilege and affirmative action.

4. Myths and Facts of Affirmation Action Activity (35 minutes)
    Ask students to provide you with a list of things that they have heard said about
    affirmative action. Write this list on newsprint or on the blackboard. Collect at least
    4-7 statements before asking students if they think any of the statements on the board
    are true. Tell each student that you will reread the statements written on the board and
    you would like then to raise they hand if they these statements to be true. Write the
    number of students who raise their hands for each statement next to it. After you have
    read through all of the students, pass out copies of the sheet below. Inform students
    that these are six commonly believe myths about affirmative action and facts
    surrounding these myths. Ask for student volunteers to read the myths and facts on
    the sheet.

Common Myths About Affirmative Action
MYTH 1: Affirmative Action is preferential treatment.
FACT: Affirmative action creates a fair competition by removing the barriers that
obstruct the lanes of women and minorities in the race toward the American Dream.
For example, because female business owners remain outside traditional old boy
networks, they often receive only a fraction of the public contracting dollars that men
do. Similarly, women and minority job seekers are frequently shut out of good jobs in
trades where opportunities go only to those who are in the loop. Efforts to ensure that
outsiders have equal access to opportunities are only fair and do not amount to
"preferential treatment."

MYTH 2: Affirmative action is no longer needed in America.
FACT: Since exclusion and unfair treatment persist in America, we need remedies to
deal with them. Affirmative action opponents turn a blind eye to the effects of race
and gender on access to opportunity. But common sense tells us that any attempt to
solve a problem by ignoring it makes no sense at all. Imagine trying to eliminate the
deadly consequences of lead poisoning by being blind to lead paint! If we want to
create opportunities that are truly equal, we need to address the barriers to
opportunity. Promoting equality and supporting affirmative action go hand in hand!

MYTH 3: Affirmative action rewards the unqualified.
FACT: The real myth is that we have an equal playing field and that the most
qualified people are the ones who get ahead. In fact, affirmative action helps to offset
barriers that unfairly block the pathways of qualified Americans who are fully able to
succeed. In so doing, it promotes equal opportunity. The world is full of people
whose talents are not always recognized by traditional measures of intelligence. For
example, although he went on to be one of the most gifted orators of the 20th century,
Dr. Martin Luther King, Jr. scored very poorly on a standardized verbal test in his
youth. Research has shown that such tests and similar criteria are often biased and
underestimate the capabilities of working class individuals, women, and people of
color, and that they do not accurately predict professional or educational success. In
countering built-in discrimination, affirmative action policies offset limited measures
of merit and identify individuals whose talents and potential might otherwise be

overlooked.

MYTH 4: Opposing affirmative action is consistent with Dr. King's dream of a colorblind America.
FACT: Dr. King and other civil rights leaders never believed that racial inequality could be fixed by ignoring the problem of racism. In fact, Dr. King supported affirmative action and advocated the use of race-conscious measures to provide opportunities for minorities.

MYTH 5: Affirmative Action only targets African Americans.
FACT: Affirmative action targets many people who continue to face opportunity barriers, including women, Native Americans, Latinos, Asian Americans, South Asians, African Americans, Arab Americans, and others. By opening fair access to more Americans, affirmative action benefits families, businesses, coworkers, communities, and our entire society.

MYTH 6: Affirmative Action should be about class, not race.
FACT: Race and gender discrimination continue to be significant problems in our country, and race- and gender conscious policies are needed to correct them. For example, a recent study showed that job applicants with "white-sounding names" were twice as likely to be called back for interviews as applicants with "black-sounding names" who had the same qualifications. Another study found that a white job applicant with a criminal record was more likely to receive a second interview than a similarly qualified African American applicant with no criminal record. Policies that address only class issues cannot address such injustices, and are not sufficient to combat the barriers limiting opportunities for racial minorities. Fortunately, many affirmative action programs do take economic status into account, so race, gender and class need not be pitted against one another in the pursuit of equality. Local decision-makers should remain free to determine the scope of affirmative action in their communities, and national campaigns should not impose a one-size-fits-all version of equality.

Source: http://www.aclu.org/images/asset_upload_file87_34806.pdf

Processing Questions:
1. How was it for you doing this activity?
2. Were these myths the same as the ones that you brainstormed as a group? What was the same? What was difference?

4. Take Aways (5 minutes): Ask students to close out the day's lesson by sharing a take away with the group. (A takeaway is a new insight or idea that they will take with them).

A Love Letter from Suheir Hammad

a call for compassion during the dissolution.
a plea for love while we learn our lessons.

i find a sense of alchemical process in the machinations of movement.
come again.

is it possible to transform truly, finally. from one identity to another?

faith, magic, revolution, love - words which feel similar when we live them. when we
somehow and impossibly will them into being, into our very beings.

after we burn away the gross and hype, what left? essence?
soul?

the scientific search for a philosopher's stone, across our various cultural histories,
depended on turning the black to white. achieving one element from another. vessels
were crafted, instruments drawn up and space made for the work. detail, trial, repetition.
a poet would find this rhythm mesmerizing, reflective. also allegorical, as our lives are
always in transition, often fragile and secretly as destructive as they are creative.

we aim to create a better world, but where the open spaces to unpack the ugly, the
history, the guilt and shame, the horror and silence, all we have accumulated through our
privilege and pain, our karma and memory? are our bodies and minds, then, the vessels
for the changes requisite? what tools do we bring to a new day?

there isn't enough space to hold all the evil man has done. there isn't enough time to get
into it. and obviously our bodies and minds have carried the experiments on our senses
through, notice how sick we are.

inherited by every generation, language corrupted. now we each decide daily what
weight, what meaning, is given words, colors, ideas. now we understand we need to burn
through the white. we were taught ideas (which are things, which shape the world) that
took us away from each other and from our selves. we are studying, gearing for the next.
we do not know what is on the other side of transformation. in america we have never not
known a white day. yet.

a love letter to your soul, on a journey towards a light never binary alone.

i wish for all we need to transform from one position to another. all the while dropping
the weight, always where it belongs, not picking up what doesn't belong to us. not other's
pain, this we hope to alleviate by right action. not other's projections, these scatter if we
see clearly.

a love letter to your soul, because we fail at loving kindness toward others when we have not mustered it for our selves.
we are students and teachers at once.

balm for your wounds as you slay your specific demons.

am so sorry for the misdirected blows.
am so thankful for the needed ones.

a letter to imagination, the only nation any of us born in.

love to courage, the only armor for the soul.

Suheir Hammad is a Palestinian-American poet, author and political activist who was born on October 1973 in Amman, Jordan to Palestinian refugee parents and immigrated with her family to Brooklyn, New York City when she was five years old.

Authors

Piper Anderson

As a theatre practitioner, author, educator, and Empowerment coach Piper Anderson has dedicated the last 10 years to holding the space for community, peace, and power to manifest. From detention facilities, public schools, and non-profits to Ivy League universities Piper Anderson is well known for her ability to dynamically engage and inspiring communities. She is a highly sought after speaker offering workshops, performances, and lectures on topics ranging from arts & activism, using popular culture as an educational tool, and mobilizing communities in ending gender violence. Just a few of the places her work has taken her include Harvard University, UC-Berkeley, University of Wisconsin-Madison, Columbia University, NYU, as well conferences such as The Tides Center's Momentum Conference, Louisiana Coalition Against Domestic Violence, Critical Resistance and New WORLD Theatres Intersections Conference. For more information visit www.piperanderson.com.

Tanesha Barnes is the Program Administrator for Diversity Education and Programming for the Center for Multicultural Education and Programs (The Center) at New York University. She has recently been selected as the 2010 Regional Outstanding New Professional Award recipient from NASPA (Student Affairs Administrators in Higher Education) Region II. She has co-facilitated various diversity workshops for groups such as NYU's Alternative Breaks Program, Residential Assistants, and summer orientation workshops for all incoming students in NYU's College of Arts and Sciences Steinhardt School of Culture, Education, and Human Development and Gallatin School of Individualized Study. She has also co-presented at various national conferences. Tanesha attended Teachers College, Columbia University for her master's degree in Higher and Postsecondary Education with a concentration in Academic and Developmental Analysis. Tanesha can be contacted at tlobarnes@gmail.com.

Andrea Dre Domingue is an educator, writer, and consultant who specializes in critical pedagogy, leadership development and student empowerment within higher education. Currently she is a pursing a doctoral degree in the Social Justice Education Concentration at the University of Massachusetts, Amherst where she also works in Leadership Education for the Department of Residence Life. In addition, Dre is a current Directorate Body member for ACPA's Commission of Social Justice Educators and also served three years as the Co-Chair for the Consortium of Higher Education LGBT Resource Professionals. Dre can be contacted at dre.domingue@gmail.com or at www.dredomingue.com.

Samantha Shapses Wertheim is an educator and administrator committed to engaging students, faculty and administrators in the practice of social justice education. Samantha received her Masters in Higher Education Administration from New York University in 2005, a Certificate in Training from New York University in 2010 and a Bachelors Degree from Washington University in St. Louis in 2001. For more information on Samantha Shapses Wertheim please visit www.samanthashapses.com.

The Creators and Editors

JLove Calderón

As an author, activist, and Certified Empowerment Facilitator, JLove has worked passionately on social justice, race, and gender issues for over 15 years. She has authored three books: We Got Issues! (New World Library, 2006) with Rha Goddess; That White Girl (Atria, 2007) which has been optioned for film; and Conscious Women Rock the Page: Using Hip-Hop Fiction to Incite Social Change (2008) with Marcella Runell Hall, E-Fierce and Black Artemis. As an activist and personal life coach, JLove has helped create practical models for living designed to empower people of all backgrounds. Her knowledge is informed by her years of working as a counselor in teen shelters, as well as teaching at El Puente Academy for Peace and Justice for over a decade. Her current projects include producing progressive film, TV, books, and educational materials that inspire new dialogue and action on behalf of peace and social justice for all. JLove graduated Cum Laude from San Diego State University with a B.A. in Africana Studies and received her Master's Degree in Education from Long Island University. For more information, please visit www.jlovecalderon.com

Marcella Runell Hall

Marcella Runell Hall is currently completing her doctoral studies in the Social Justice Education Program at the University of Massachusetts, Amherst. Her dissertation is entitled: Education in a Hip-Hop Nation: Identity, Politics and Pedagogy. Marcella has worked as a freelance writer for the New York Times Learning Network and VIBE magazine. Marcella regularly presents her work at national conferences, colleges and universities and community-based events. Marcella co-edited two books, The Hip-Hop Education Guidebook (2007) with Martha Diaz and Conscious Women Rock the Page: Using Hip-Hop Fiction to Incite Social Change (2008) with JLove, E-Fierce and Black Artemis. Additionally she has written many essays and articles, as well as a literacy book entitled Ten Most Influential Hip-Hop Artists (Scholastic 2008). She has received many awards for teaching and writing about social justice and diversity including the prestigious American Association of Colleges &University's K. Patricia Cross Future Scholar Award and as well as a Racial Unity Citation from the Brooklyn Borough President's Office. Marcella is currently the Associate Director of Multicultural Education and Programs for New York University. For more information please visit: www.marcellarhall.com

CPSIA information can be obtained at www.ICGtesting.com
Printed in the USA
LVOW020910130613

338397LV00007B/616/P